THE ILLUSTRATED HISTORY OF THE WORLD

The Modern World

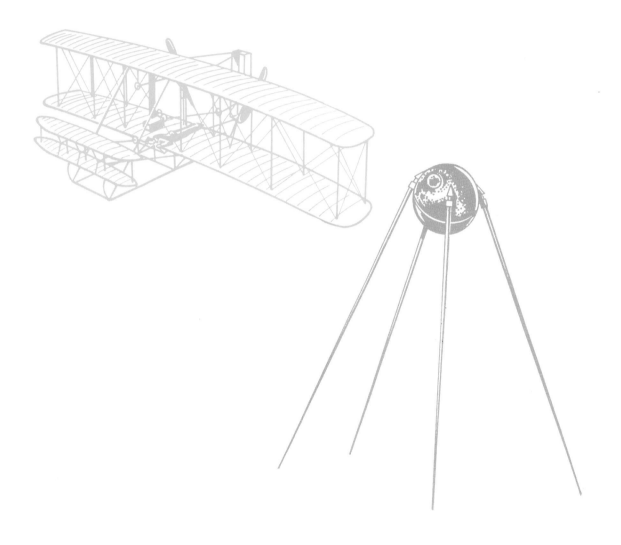

PREFACE

*T*he Illustrated History of the World is a unique series of eight volumes covering the entire scope of human history, from the days of the nomadic hunters up to the present. Each volume surveys significant events and personages, key political and economic developments, and the critical forces that inspired change, in both institutions and the everyday life of people around the globe.

The books are organized on a spread-by-spread basis, allowing ease of access and depth of coverage on a wide range of fascinating topics and time periods within any one volume. Each spread serves as a kind of mini-essay, in words and pictures, of its subject. The text—cogent, concise and lively—is supplemented by an impressive array of illustrations (original art, full-color photographs, maps, diagrams) and features (glossary, index, time charts, further reading listings). Taking into account the new emphasis on multicultural education, special care has been given to presenting a balanced portrait of world history: the volumes in the series explore all civilizations— whether it's the Mayans in Mexico, the Shoguns in Japan or the Sumerians in the Middle East.

The Modern World

.

Stephen Hoare

☑
Facts On File

Facts On File, Inc.
460 Park Avenue South
New York NY 10016

Library of Congress Cataloging-in-Publication Data

Hoare, Stephen.
The modern world / Stephen Hoare.
p.   cm.
(The illustrated history of the world)
Includes bibliographical references and index.
Summary: Discusses the decline of the old European empires, the
world wars, scientific advances, new religious and cultural ideas,
and other changes that have occurred during the twentieth century.
ISBN 0-8160-2792-7
1. History, Modern—20th century—Juvenile literature.
[1. History, Modern—20th century.] I. Title. II. Series:
Illustrated history of the world (New York, N.Y.)
D421.H58 1993
909.82—dc20
92-2405
CIP
AC

ISBN 0 8160 2792 7

Facts On File books are available at special discounts when purchased
in bulk quantities for businesses, associations, institutions or sales
promotions. Please call our Special Sales Department in New York at
212/683-2244 (dial 800/322-8755 except in NY, AK or HI).

Designed by Hammond Hammond
Composition by Goodfellow and Egan Ltd, Cambridge
Printed and Bound by BPCC Hazell Books, Paulton and Aylesbury

10 9 8 7 6 5 4 3 2 1

This book is printed on acid-free paper.

First Published in Great Britain in 1991 by
Simon and Schuster Young Books

CONTENTS

INTRODUCTION

If you ask anyone which period of history they know the most about, they will probably say the twentieth century. Newspapers and television give very vivid accounts of wars and major political events around the world today. Current events quickly become history.

Your parents and relatives will remember many things about life when they were young, and photographs and household objects from earlier days can bring the past to life. Yet the present century can be very difficult to understand because its history is being updated all the time.

Divisions and *alliances* between nations are changing constantly and it is very difficult to make any clear predictions about the future. Sometimes new events make us look at the past in a different way. For example, the break-up of the Soviet Union in late 1991 could be seen as the end of a chapter that started with the Russian Revolution of 1917.

In Part One of this book, you will read about the twentieth century up to the end of World War II. In the developed nations, there were great technological changes, speeded by the development of mass communications such as the telephone and the radio, and helped by industrial *mass production*. These not only improved people's everyday lives, but also extended the power of nations to wage war.

In Part Two, you will see how victory for the Allies in 1945 resulted in the United States of America and the Soviet Union developing as *superpowers*. Their nuclear technology developed rapidly and led to an arms race in which neither side had a clear advantage and an uneasy *balance of power* was maintained. But Britain and the older colonial powers of Europe were weakened after the war and could no longer keep control of their colonies in Africa and Asia. The later years of the twentieth century saw countries in the developing world struggle to achieve democracy and escape from poverty.

Today a critical challenge for the world is to find ways of saving the planet from the damage that people's activities have done to the environment.

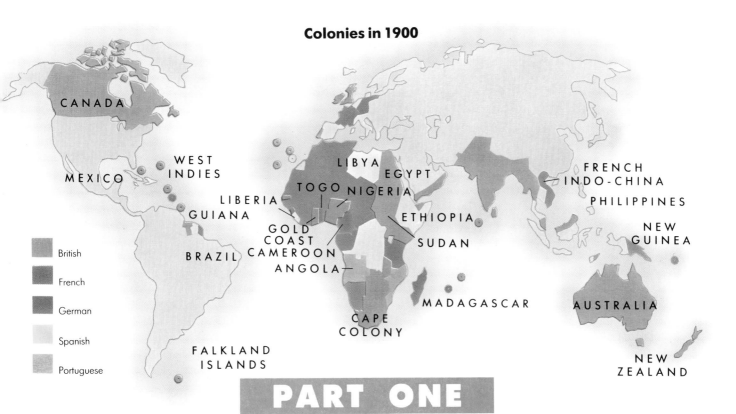

Colonies in 1900

CANADA

WEST INDIES

MEXICO

LIBERIA

GUIANA

BRAZIL

GOLD COAST

CAMEROON

ANGOLA

FALKLAND ISLANDS

LIBYA

TOGO NIGERIA

EGYPT

ETHIOPIA

SUDAN

CAPE COLONY

MADAGASCAR

FRENCH INDO-CHINA

PHILIPPINES

NEW GUINEA

AUSTRALIA

NEW ZEALAND

British

French

German

Spanish

Portuguese

PART ONE

The End of the Old Order

At the beginning of the twentieth century, many areas of the world were ruled by the old colonial powers of Europe, such as Britain, France, Belgium and the Netherlands, which had built up empires during the previous century. However, Germany and Italy, each of which had only become a united country in the second half of the nineteenth century, had very few colonies and little world influence.

RIVALRY BETWEEN BRITAIN AND GERMANY The wealthiest and most successful colonial nation was Britain. It had a tiny army but a large navy, and was powerful enough to govern an empire which included Canada and Australia, the Indian subcontinent and several African states. After 1900, Germany's growing industrial strength led to rivalry with Britain. This found expression in the race to build bigger and better fleets of battleships.

RUSSIA In eastern Europe, the tsars of Russia governed a huge but backward empire which had

scarcely been touched by modern agricultural techniques or industrialization. The extreme poverty of many of the Russian people helped the *Marxist* revolution of 1917 to succeed.

TWO WORLD WARS Within western Europe, Germany's alliance with the old Austro-Hungarian Empire posed a threat to neighboring countries such as France and Belgium in the west and Russia in the east. It was clearly only a matter of time before Europe's old order was destroyed. The war that broke out in 1914 quickly spread to the Middle East and involved Turkey's Ottoman Empire as well.

People called the First World War the "war to end all wars," but within 20 years war had broken out again. The years between the two wars had seen the growth of *dictatorships* in Germany, Italy and Spain. They were helped by the great poverty and discontent in these countries. During this time, Japan also increased its military power and threatened the colonial interests of Britain and the USA.

9

OLD EMPIRES AND NEW POWERS

Major changes were on the way at the beginning of the twentieth century. Empires which had lasted for centuries were about to break up, and other nations were becoming more powerful.

THE BRITISH EMPIRE In 1900 the most powerful country was Britain, which ruled an empire that covered a quarter of the world. This empire included India, much of central and southern Africa, the West Indies, Hong Kong and Malaysia. Britain's biggest *colonies*, Canada and Australia, had their own governments but the British monarch still had the final say in what happened there.

Britain had not had to fight a major war since the end of the Napoleonic Wars in 1815. However, between 1899 and 1902 British troops fought and won a war against Dutch *Boer* settlers for control of South Africa.

EMPIRES IN DECLINE The two old empires of eastern Europe, Austria-Hungary and Russia, were now becoming weaker. Austria-Hungary was made up of different peoples, such as the Slovaks, Slavs and Czechs, who all wanted to be independent. Other states such as Serbia also wanted to break away from Austria's influence.

Russia was by far the largest empire of the old world, but now it was facing problems too. Russia's leader, the

Europe in 1914

Alliances and treaties between groups of nations form power blocks across continents. Sometimes this can threaten the stability of a continent such as Europe.

GREAT BRITAIN

GERMAN EMPIRE

RUSSIA

FRANCE

AUSTRIA HUNGARY

ITALY

MEDITERRANEAN

Triple Alliance

Triple Entente

The Dreadnoughts

In February 1906, the Royal Navy launched a new kind of battleship, the Dreadnought. This new ship was thickly armored and carried ten 12-inch (30-cm) guns. It was powered by steam turbines, giving it a top speed of an impressive 21 knots (nautical miles per hour). The armament was enormous in comparison to the warships of the nineteenth century. Under Admiral John Fischer, the Navy built more and more of the new Dreadnoughts.

The German navy began to enter the arms race too, and by 1914 Britain led Germany in the numbers of large warships, 117 to 87. For most of the war these great ships stayed in harbor because both sides thought them too precious to lose. They met once, at the Battle of Jutland in the North Sea on May 31, 1916. The results were inconclusive and both fleets retired, never to leave port again.

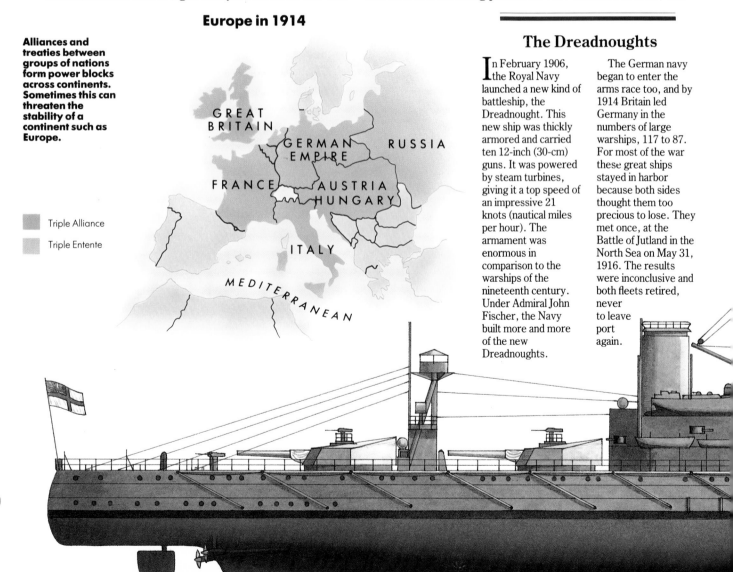

tsar, was an emperor who ruled over a country that covered one-sixth of the Earth's land surface. But, although it was so big, the industrial revolution which had transformed most of western Europe had made little difference to Russia. It was a backward *feudal society* which depended on farming and which was run in an old-fashioned, inefficient way.

Groups of Marxists, who wanted to bring changes to Russia, organized the opposition to Tsar Nicholas II (1894–1917). In 1905 they tried to launch a revolution against him. Nicholas then set up an assembly of representatives who were elected by the middle classes to help govern the country. This move towards *democracy* was not enough to prevent a revolution in 1917 (see pages 24–25).

Turkey's great Ottoman Empire was also in decline, but it still ruled over Greece, Palestine and Mesopotamia (present-day Iraq). In 1908 junior officers in the Turkish army, known as the "young Turks," overthrew the unpopular Sultan Abdul Hamid II and set up a western European–style government.

Right. Japan flexes its industrial muscles in a territorial war against the declining Russian empire.

RISING POWERS

The United States of America and Japan were two new powers that were about to challenge the domination of the old empires. In 1894 Japan had defeated China and had seized land around Port Arthur, in northern China near to its border with Russia. In a war against Russia in 1904, the Japanese navy sank the entire Russian Baltic fleet at the Battle of Tsushima.

The United States had recently seized the Philippines and Cuba from Spain. In 1903 it used a revolution in Panama as an excuse to take control of that country from Colombia, so clearing the way for the building of the Panama Canal.

In 1870 the Prussian leader, Bismarck, had united all the different German states into one empire. By 1900, this was the strongest industrial power in Europe. Its growing influence caused the great empires and nations of Europe to group together in different alliances.

NEW ALLIANCES

Germany, Austria-Hungary and Italy formed the Triple Alliance to protect themselves from possible attack by France or Russia. France and Russia joined to form the Dual Entente. In 1904 Britain and France signed the Entente Cordiale, agreeing to help each other in time of war. Europe was ready for a major war.

Above. In 1904, Britain's alliance with France, the Entente Cordiale, settled the two countries' colonial disputes in North Africa and they agreed to help each **other in time of war. But the entente provoked Germany into challenging their influence in Morocco. This postcard is a memento of the alliance, and shows** **President Fallières of France and King Edward VII.**

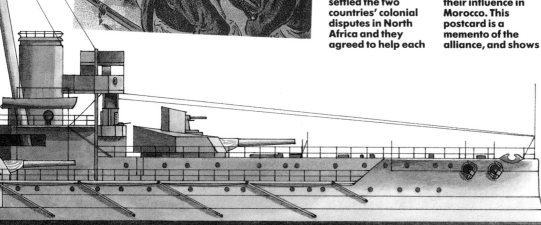

Left. *HMS Dreadnought*. Built in 1904, this revolutionary battleship was the first to use steam turbines. It carried ten 12-inch (30-cm) guns and was faster than any other warship. It protected Britain's sea trade and was a major deterrent against enemy aggression.

TECHNOLOGICAL DEVELOPMENTS

The calm water of harbors promised smooth landings for the large passenger-carrying flying boats of the 1930s, although their popularity soon began to wane.

Great technological changes took place at the beginning of the twentieth century. These developments, particularly in the areas of transport and communications, began to touch on and improve the lives of ordinary people more than ever before.

Technological progress was regarded as a good and necessary thing. There were no worries about the pollution caused by factories and no one thought that supplies of fuels like coal or gas would ever run out.

TRANSPORT The motor car was developed towards the end of the nineteenth century. At first it was an expensive luxury that only the rich could afford. But new methods of making large numbers of items, known as *mass-production* techniques, were developed by Henry Ford in the US, and this made cars more affordable.

Cars had been developed after the *internal combustion engine* was invented in 1876. This engine also made powered flight possible. In 1900, a German called Count Zeppelin built a huge gas-filled airship that was powered by two gasoline engines. On December 17, 1903, Orville Wright took to the air in an airplane made of wood and canvas at Kitty Hawk, South Carolina.

World War I (see pages 16–23) encouraged the development of fighter airplanes and bombers. In 1919, two British pilots, Alcock and Brown, made the first flight across the Atlantic Ocean in a Vickers Vimy bomber that had been adapted to fly the long distance.

By the early 1920s, private airlines were advertising regular passenger flights from London to the main European cities. However, for most people, going by sea was still the only way of traveling to another continent.

In the 1930s, airships began regular flights across the Atlantic. But when the German airship *Hindenburg* burst into flames at Lakehurst, New Jersey, in 1936, people lost confidence in this form of transport.

NEW COMMUNICATIONS The telephone and the phonograph (record player) had been invented in the late nineteenth century.

The Italian electrical engineer Guglielmo Marconi invented wireless telegraphy in 1895. This allowed Morse signals – dots and dashes – to be sent over long distances and was mainly used to send messages between ships. But in 1906 an American, Reginald Fessenden, sent continuous waves of sound by wireless. Words and music could be broadcast for the first time.

RADIO, CINEMA AND TELEVISION In Britain, the British Broadcasting Company (BBC) was set up in 1922. Radio was no longer just for the rich, because a radio receiver, a "crystal set," could be made simply and cheaply at home.

The cinema was also developing rapidly. *The Jazz Singer* (1927) was the first talking picture ever made. Audiences were amazed to hear the film's star, Al Jolson, speak the first famous words: *"You ain't seen nothing yet!"*

The first television system was demonstrated by a Scottish scientist, John Logie Baird, as early as 1926. Ten years later the BBC began regular television broadcasts from Alexandra Palace in London.

The airship *Hindenburg* explodes while docking at Lakehurst, New Jersey. There were no survivors.

Landmarks of Speed and Distance

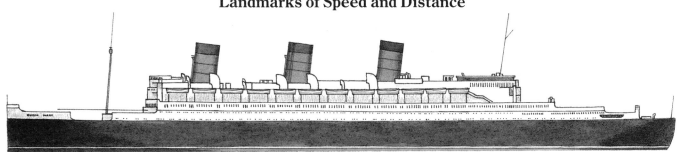

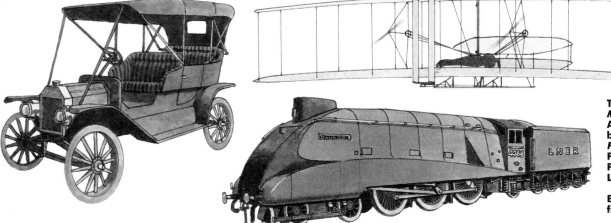

Top. The *Queen Mary*.
Above. The Wright brothers' biplane *Flyer 3*.
Far left. Model T Ford.
Left. The *Mallard*.

Below. One of the first telephones.

December 17, 1903, Orville Wright makes the world's first powered flight in an aircraft, flying 120 feet (36.5m) in 12 seconds.
July 25, 1909, Louis Blériot makes the first flight across the English Channel.
July 14–15, 1919, Capt. John Alcock and Lt. Arthur Whitten Brown make the first Atlantic flight.

1919 The world's first daily international airline service started by Aircraft Transport and Travel Ltd., from Hounslow, England, to Le Bourget, France.
July 21, 1925, Malcolm Campbell, in 350 horsepower Sunbeam *Bluebird*, is the first to reach 385 mi per hour on land.
May 21, 1927 Charles Lindbergh

makes the first solo Atlantic flight.
1929 German airship *Graf Zeppelin* completes a round-the-world trip.
May 5–24, 1930 Amy Johnson flies solo from Britain to Australia.
1935 Sir Malcolm Campbell, in *Bluebird* 3, breaks the land speed record, reaching a speed of 775 mi per hour.

1937 The *Queen Mary* breaks the Atlantic crossing record in 3 days, 20 hours and 42 minutes.
1938 *Mallard* reaches a speed of 323 mi per hour pulling seven coaches.

Key Dates in Transport

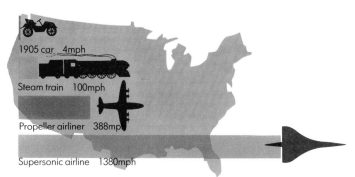

1905 car 4mph
Steam train 100mph
Propeller airliner 388mph
Supersonic airline 1380mph

The development of transport in this century has been astonishing. *Concorde* can now travel across the US in under two hours.

5000 BC	Pack animals first used
1500 BC	First wheeled vehicle, in Mesopotamia
900 AD	Chinese invent canals and canal locks
100	Compass reaches Europe
1522	First circumnavigation of the globe, expedition led by Magellan
1783	Montgolfier brothers make first flight in hot-air balloon
1816	Tarmacadam roads
1829	Stephenson's Rocket
1885	Daimler develops practical internal combustion engine
1903	Wright brothers make first controlled airplane flight
1937	Jet engine invented
1947	First plane to break the sound barrier
1959	The first hovercraft built
1961	Yuri Gagarin, first man in space
1969	Neil Armstrong, first man on the Moon

SCIENTIFIC IDEAS AND THE ARTS

At the beginning of the twentieth century, new scientific ideas and new movements in art, literature and music reflected the excitement and optimism which people felt as they entered a new century.

SCIENCE Scientists began to question the nature of the world around them and some very important theories were developed at this time. Albert Einstein's Theory of Relativity, published in 1905, explained one of the key secrets of the universe, which was that the smallest particle—the atom—contained an enormous amount of "locked up" energy. At first it was thought that this energy could never be released, but in 1919 British scientist Ernest Rutherford used radioactivity to split a nitrogen atom. This led to the development of nuclear energy and, eventually, to the making of an atomic bomb.

THE MIND Equally important developments occurred in psychology—the study of how the human mind works. Sigmund Freud, an Austrian doctor, used hypnosis to find out his patients' deepest thoughts. He developed a system called *psychoanalysis* to help cure some forms of mental illness.

The increasing knowledge of psychology had an effect on literature and art. Writers like Marcel Proust, James Joyce and Virginia Woolf explored the innermost thoughts of the characters they wrote about, while playwrights like Henrik Ibsen used the theater to show the problems that can arise between people.

The artists Pablo Picasso and Georges Braque led a movement called *cubism*, in which an object was seen from many different angles at the same time. Instead of

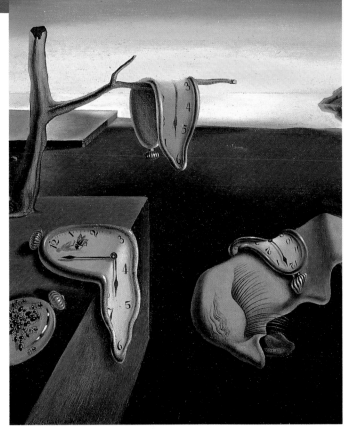

Salvador Dali's dream-like painting, *The Persistence of Memory* (1931), is a surrealist painting. Its dream-like imagery is represented in sharp focus and as realistically as possible, almost resembling color photography.

Austrian scientist Albert Einstein's theories about the atom heralded the dawning of the nuclear age and completely changed the way we think about the universe and how it works.

painting something exactly as it was, they wanted to show the ideas and feelings that could be expressed about it. Other artists included *surrealists* like Salvador Dali and Rene Magritte, whose paintings show a disturbing dream world where anything could happen.

ENTERTAINMENT, DESIGN AND ARCHITECTURE

Throughout the 1920s and 1930s, the gramophone (record player), wireless (radio) and cinema became available to more people. New forms of entertainment were dominated by the USA. Hollywood became the world capital of film-making. Jazz, a type of music developed by blacks in the American southern states, was popular all over the world and it also influenced classical composers like George Gershwin.

Modern designs, included *Art Deco*, which got its name from the Paris Exposition des Arts Decoratifs of 1925. It took the idea of streamlining used on planes,

Left. Completed in 1930, New York's Chrysler Building shows the influence of Art Deco in architecture. The decorations represent the rising sun, a popular basis for designs. Stylized flowers and zig-zag motifs were also common.

Sigmund Freud

Sigmund Freud (1856–1939) developed the theory of psychoanalysis, a way of treating people's mental disorders by encouraging them to a talk openly about their hidden thoughts. He was an Austrian doctor who worked mainly in Vienna. He drew up his theory after hearing of a Dr. Breur who had cured hysteria by hypnotizing his patients so that they remembered an important event in their life that was buried. They could then begin to understand it and the illness could be cured.

Freud found that not all illnesses could be treated using hypnosis, so he got his patients to talk about their lives in general, and particularly their childhoods.

He also believed that sexual impulses hold the key to human behavior, even from our earliest years. He was criticized by

some doctors because they did not understand his approach and because many of his patients were rich, neurotic, Viennese women who did not represent a cross section of society. Freud has done much to help us understand how our minds operate.

He wrote many papers and books, one of the most famous being *The Interpretation of Dreams*, which suggests that the subconscious mind is expressed in dreams.

1 Venustiana Carranzo became president of Mexico in 1914 but soon fell out with his lieutenant and civil war and chaos followed. In 1915 Carranzo was recognized as the president by the United States. Local difficulties led in 1916 to the US Army mounting raids in Mexico, which were not greatly successful.

2 In 1908 a constitutional convention was held to discuss the future of South Africa. The convention decided that the states, including Natal, Cape Colony, Orange River Colony and Transvaal, should form a union. English and Dutch became the official languages and the head of the Union was the king of the United Kingdom.

Below. Colorful Art Deco ceramic designs by Clarice Cliff are now highly prized by collectors. Art Deco relied on strong colors that were influenced by nature. They had shapes that reflected the new streamlined trains and airplanes.

trains and cars, and applied it to everyday objects such as radios, telephones and furniture. These designers used modern materials, such as tubular chrome and an early type of plastic called bakelite, in their work.

In the world of architecture, the techniques of building with steel frames and reinforced concrete made it possible to build tall structures, such as the skyscrapers of New York. When the Empire State Building was completed in 1931 it became, at 1,472 feet (449m), the tallest skyscraper in the world. It kept this record until 1973.

The French architect Le Corbusier put forward the idea of people living in high-rise blocks that contained apartments, shops and recreation areas. His Unit d'Habitation was built in Marseilles in France in 1946 and became the model for housing developments in the second half of the century.

World War I

OUTBREAK OF WAR

Austrian Archduke Francis Ferdinand is shot in Sarajevo, Serbia. His assassin Princep is led away.

In the early years of the twentieth century, many people believed that the peace in Europe was only temporary. Germany was rapidly becoming a major economic and military power, and some of the older empires saw it as a threat.

France was particularly worried. It had suffered a humiliating defeat in the Franco-Prussian War of 1870. Prussia, one of the largest independent states that had later combined to form Germany, had taken the important industrial region of Alsace-Lorraine from the French.

ALLIANCES AND ARMAMENTS France and Russia had agreed in August 1891 that if either country was attacked, the other would give it full military support. In 1904 Britain had made separate agreements with Russia and France, also promising its support if there was a war. In eastern Europe, Russia wanted to prevent the expansion of Germany's ally, the Austro-Hungarian Empire.

Every major European country began to spend more and more money building bigger and better equipped armies and navies. It

The most successful advertising campaign of all time: Lord Kitchener's appeals recruit a huge army of volunteers.

needed only one small incident to upset the balance of power and spark off a war.

On June 28, 1914, Archduke Francis Ferdinand of Austria was murdered in Sarajevo in Serbia, as a protest against Austrian control of that country. The Austro-Hungarian Empire immediately declared war on Serbia. Russia came to Serbia's aid and ordered its army to prepare for war. Now the leaders of Germany became anxious. If Russia invaded Austria-Hungary, then it might also attack Germany. France, Russia's ally, might seize the opportunity to attack Germany from the west.

THE VON SCHLIEFFEN PLAN In 1905, the chief of staff of the German army, Count Alfred von Schlieffen, had drawn up a plan to deal with this situation. As Russia was so vast, it would take about two weeks after it had declared war before it was ready to fight, because Russian troops would have to travel long distances to reach the *front line*, where the fighting was. The plan was to use this time to send most of the German army through Belgium to attack France from the north.

The German army would surround Paris and force the French army to fight a defensive battle that it would be certain to lose. By the time Russia could equip its army and send it into battle, France would have surrendered and Germany's entire army would be free to concentrate on a war in the east.

WAR IS DECLARED On August 1, 1914, Germany declared war on Russia. Two days later it declared war on France and sent its army through Belgium to attack. Because it had agreed in 1830 to defend Belgium if it was invaded, Britain declared war on Germany on August 4.

Throughout the 1914–1918 war, most of the fighting was in France and Belgium and on the borders of Russia. Nevertheless, the war was called a world war because fighting spread to eastern Europe, Turkey and the Middle East. In 1917, the United States entered the conflict (see pages 22–23). Indian, Canadian and Australian regiments also fought with the British.

BRITONS

"WANTS"

YOU

JOIN YOUR COUNTRY'S ARMY!

GOD SAVE THE KING

Industrial power. This photograph shows a German armaments factory in full production at the beginning of World War I. The Germans increased their stores of weapons as all countries prepared for war.

The Size of Regular Armies in 1914

GREAT BRITAIN	580		RUSSIA	5,000,000	
FRANCE	339		FRANCE	4,000,000	
			GREAT BRITAIN	300,000	
RUSSIA	167		BELGIUM	300,000	
			SERBIA	300,000	
GERMANY	327		GERMANY	5,000,000	
AUSTRIA	115		AUSTRIA	2,500,000	

The sizes of the armies ranged against each other at the beginning of World War I differed in the relative importance attached to the army as compared to the navy. No air forces were in operation at this time but the types that would form the early warplanes were being developed. France,

Russia and Germany all had large standing armies. The French lost many of their men in the early days of the war at Verdun, where they held up the German advance at a cost of 300,000 casualties. The British had only a small standing army, which was swelled in the days to come by volunteers,

encouraged by Lord Kitchener. The largest navy was the British Navy, which had entered a ship-building war with the Germans. These great navies met only once, at the Battle of Jutland. The stalemate trench warfare meant that many men were needed to replace those lost at the front.

Germany Invades, August 1914

Right. Von Schlieffen's famous plan was drawn up to combat the possibility of attack on two fronts. Once the French had surrendered, Germany would then move its troops to the east ready to defend its border with Russia.

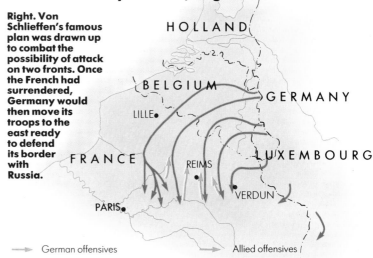

→ German offensives   → Allied offensives

Austro-Hungarian Empire 1914

A map of Austria-Hungary at the beginning of World War I. The empire did not survive the war.

After 1867 administered from Vienna

After 1867 administered from Budapest

After 1908, joint Austro-Hungarian administration

THE WAR IN EUROPE

At first, the war was fought by armies on the move. *Allied forces* had to move quickly to stop the German army's rapid advance. Some early battles were fought by cavalry, i.e., soldiers on horseback.

On August 12, a force of 81,472 British soldiers and 30,000 horses set out for France under the command of General Sir John French. In Britain, people believed that the war would be over by Christmas. After several minor battles with German forces, the British stopped the German advance at Ypres in Belgium in mid-October. Meanwhile, the French army halted the German forces in the valleys of the Somme and the Marne rivers.

TRENCH WARFARE All across western Europe, from the Belgian coast to Switzerland, the opposing armies dug lines of trenches to mark out the territory they had gained. These lines of trenches became known as the Western Front. The ground in between them was called "no man's land."

Gradually, the trench systems were enlarged and fortified to make them harder to attack. Thousands of soldiers were needed to defend them. From the shelter of a trench, one soldier with a machine-gun could mow down hundreds of advancing troops. To attack a well-defended enemy trench meant almost certain death.

The Western Front 1914–1918

Spectacular German advances in 1914 forced the Allies to counter attack in the Battle of the Marne. Throughout the war Allies and Germans fought a series of battles around the Belgian town of Ypres to prevent the Germans breaking through the Allied lines along the Channel coast. 1916 saw a massive German attack against the French fortress of Verdun.

Furthest German advance

Area of fiercest fighting

++++ Cease-fire

·········· Front in 1918

---- Front in 1914

THE GENERALS' WAR Nevertheless, generals on both sides thought that they could only make progress if they launched massive attacks on the enemy's trenches. In almost every case these attacks failed. Two of the biggest and most disastrous battles came in 1916. On February 21, the German army attacked the French fortress of Verdun. Although the French were heavily outnumbered, General Pétain ordered his troops to fight to the last man. As the number of French casualties rose, Pétain sent in more and more troops.

For four months the French army held on to the fortress, although the German attacks had reduced it to ruins. In the end the Germans gave up. They had lost about 218,000 men. But the French had lost 315,000. The French army had not given way but its spirit was broken. On July 1, the British and French launched a combined attack in the valley of the Somme which was to last until November. Troops carrying heavy equipment and moving across open ground were easy targets for the German machine-gunners. On the first day of the battle, 20,000 British soldiers were killed and another 40,000 were wounded, the highest casualties suffered in a single day of the war.

WEARING DOWN THE ENEMY As the war went on, countries *conscripted*, ordered to join the army, huge numbers of men. Allied generals liked large battles because they thought that eventually the Germans would run out of soldiers. In fact, the populations of Germany and its allies were growing, and they had more than enough men to replace those who died. The military power of the Allies was not enough to end the war quickly.

Down the line from death. Wounded British soldiers make their way to a field hospital.

In Flanders Fields

In Flanders fields the poppies blow
Between the crosses, row on row
 That mark our place; and in the sky
 The larks, still bravely singing, fly
Scarce heard amid the guns below.

We are the Dead. Short days ago
We lived, felt dawn, saw sunset glow,
 Loved and were loved, and now we lie
 In Flanders fields.

Take up our quarrel with the foe:
To you from failing hands we throw
 The torch; be yours to hold it high.
 If ye break faith with us who die
We shall not sleep, though poppies grow
 In Flanders fields.

John McCrae, Died in Base Hospital, 1918

The last great disaster for the Allies was the Battle of Passchendaele, near Ypres, which started on July 31, 1917. Rain and the heavy bombardment of shells had turned the battlefield to mud. During two and a half months of fighting, British troops suffered 300,000 casualties and the German casualties were 275,000 men.

The Introduction of Tanks

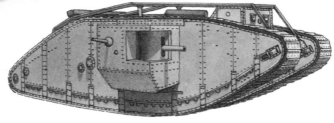

In October 1917, British troops won a minor but significant victory against the Germans at Cambrai, northern France, when they launched a surprise attack using tanks.

The tank was a new weapon which changed twentieth-century warfare

completely. It was an armor-plated vehicle with caterpillar tracks which enabled it to move slowly but steadily across rough terrain. The tank had cannons which could fire to the front and to the side.

The sheer size and weight of the tank meant that it could

break through the tangled barbed-wire fortifications protecting the German trenches. Foot soldiers following behind the tanks were protected from enemy fire and could move through the gaps created in the barbed wire.

Left.
Soldiers lived their daily lives in the comparative safety of a trench while waiting for orders to go into battle. If the enemy started shelling the trench, soldiers would have to shelter underground in dugouts.

WAR ON ALL FRONTS

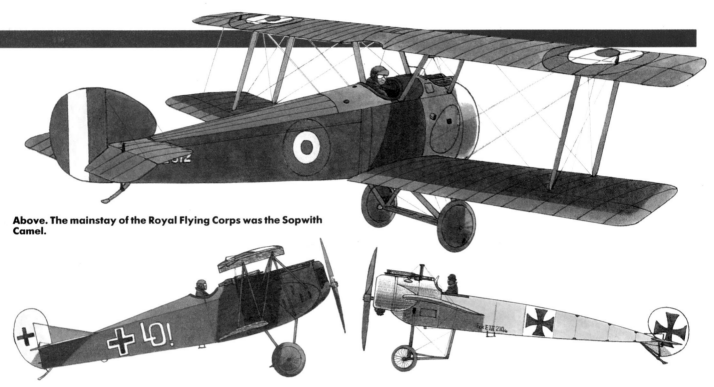

Above. The mainstay of the Royal Flying Corps was the Sopwith Camel.

A German Fokker D7 biplane.

Another German fighter, this time a Fokker E1 monoplane, an advance on the earlier models.

World War I was fought in eastern Europe and the Middle East as well as in Belgium and France.

THE EASTERN FRONT Russia was not well-prepared for war. Now that France and Britain were fighting Germany on the Western Front, Russia moved quickly to support its allies and sent troops into eastern Germany. But the Germans won a decisive victory at the Battle of Tannenburg on August 29, 1914. The remaining Russian forces retreated.

Meanwhile, a third Russian army had suffered heavy losses when it had attacked and defeated the Austrians. Germany sent reinforcements to Austria and succeeded in turning back the Russian advance. The eastern borders of Germany and Austria were now safe from further attack, and so Germany was able to strengthen its attack in the west.

The Germans, who had planned to defeat France quickly so that their armies could fight off a massive Russian attack, found that they could easily fight a war on two borders after all. On May 2, 1915 they attacked Russia along a wide stretch of the Eastern Front and in the middle of the year Germany captured most of Poland, which had previously been controlled by Russia.

Italy joined the Allies on May 23, 1915, by declaring war on Austria-Hungary. This meant that Austrian troops had to leave the Russian front to defend Austria's mountainous southern border with Italy.

TURKEY In October 1914 Turkey entered the war as an ally of Germany and immediately sent an army to attack Russia. Thousands of Turks died in this campaign as a result of the bitterly cold Russian winter.

Turkey's empire included a large part of the Middle East and so it was in a good position to cut off supplies of oil to the Allies. Turkey also threatened to attack the Suez Canal, which would prevent supplies reaching Britain from Australia and India.

One way of hitting at Turkey was to prevent German supplies reaching Turkey through the *Balkan states* of southeastern Europe. A British and French force landed at Salonika in Greece, which was *neutral*, not part of the war. They hoped to join up with the Serbian army and prevent any reinforcements from Germany or Austria-Hungary reaching Turkey.

This Allied army was unable to prevent the defeat of Serbia by the Austro-Hungarian army, which went on to conquer the Balkan states of Montenegro and Albania. In the end it seemed that the Allied army had served no useful function in this area and had simply drawn troops

Gallipoli

Australian and New Zealand (ANZAC) troops land at Gallipoli in 1915.

Turkey controlled the narrow straits of the Bosphorus, and so cut off Russia's most direct sea route to the west. With this route closed, the Allies found it impossible to send supplies to Russia.

In order to distract Turkish troops from attacking Russia, Britain sent a naval force to land troops at Gallipoli on Turkey's Aegean coast. The first landings took place on April 25, 1915. Australian and New Zealand troops (ANZACs) were used as part of the first attack. They suffered heavy losses when they tried to climb the steep cliffs.

The Gallipoli campaign was badly managed from the start. Allied troops suffered appalling casualties and gained little or nothing. They never succeeded in taking the well-defended Turkish positions on the cliff tops, and on January 8, 1916, British commanders organized a safe withdrawal to ships waiting offshore.

The Eastern Front 1914–1918

Below. The war on the eastern front. The Germans won decisive battles at Tannenburg (Aug 1914), and at the battle of the Masurian Lakes (Sept 1914), completely destroying two Russian armies. Winter prevented a further German advance. In a second great offensive in 1915 the German army captured the whole of Poland and Lithuania leaving one million Russian soldiers dead. After the Bolshevik Revolution of 1917, Russia was forced to pull out of the war, leaving the Germans in possession of a huge part of western Russia.

The Central Powers

Neutral states

Turkey Defeated 1917–1918

The map shows the Allied advances towards Turkey during the First World War from Palestine in the west and from Mesopotamia (present-day Iraq) in the east.

→ Arab attacks

→ British advance

→ French naval landings

Occupied by Britain 1–3 Nov. 1918 to stop a French occupation

Occupied by Britain 1914–1918

Under Turkish control 1918

away from the Western Front, where they were badly needed.

THE MIDDLE EAST The British landed a small army in Palestine to protect the Suez Canal from a Turkish attack. This campaign is best remembered for the heroic actions of Colonel T. E. Lawrence—Lawrence of Arabia—who organized a secret *resistance movement* among the Palestinians, encouraging them to fight the Turks who governed their country.

British forces led by General Allenby advanced against the Turks and on December 9, 1917, drove them out of Jerusalem. Prime Minister Lloyd George announced that Britain intended to create a Jewish homeland in Palestine when the war ended.

Colonel T. E. Lawrence adopted the headgear of the Arab resistance fighters with whom he joined forces.

AMERICA ENTERS THE WAR

At first, the United States was neutral in the First World War. But the Allies were able to buy essential supplies and weapons from America. These supplies had to be sent across the Atlantic by ship.

GERMANY'S U-BOAT BLOCKADE

In early 1915, Germany declared a *blockade* of Britain. This meant that it tried to prevent ships going in and out of British ports. It also announced that its submarines (U-boats) would sink any British *merchant ship* they saw.

Germany's war on merchant shipping hit the US's export trade hard. US ships were sunk and the lives of its citizens were also placed in danger. About 100 Americans died when the British liner *Lusitania* was sunk

DEFEND YOUR COUNTRY

ENLIST NOW *in the* **UNITED STATES ARMY**

An American recruitment poster showing Uncle Sam preparing for a bare knuckle fight with the enemy.

by a U-boat off the coast of Ireland in May 1915. Germany's U-boat campaign helped prepare public opinion in the USA for war.

On January 31, 1917, Germany announced that it would step up its U-boat war to include any ships from neutral countries that it found in the eastern Atlantic. On April 6, after protests about US ships being sunk, the US declared war on Germany.

It would take time for America to raise an army of volunteers, equip them and send them to France. In the meantime, the US lent money and supplies freely to the Allies. With the industrial might of the US on the side of the Allies, Germany could not hope to win.

HUNGER AND REVOLUTION

Throughout the summer of 1917 there were food riots in Petrograd (St. Petersburg) in Russia. The advancing German armies had captured the rich farming land of Ukraine. Soon Russia would be overtaken by revolution and would leave the war (see pages 24–25).

But there were also food shortages in Germany. Britain's powerful navy had kept up a blockade to prevent imports reaching German ports. Germany's farms were

The New York Times.
EXTRA 5:30 A.M.

LUSITANIA SUNK BY A SUBMARINE, PROBABLY 1,260 DEAD;
TWICE TORPEDOED OFF IRISH COAST; SINKS IN 15 MINUTES;
CAPT. TURNER SAVED, FROHMAN AND VANDERBILT MISSING;
WASHINGTON BELIEVES THAT A GRAVE CRISIS IS AT HAND

Left. The sinking of the *Lusitania* with death of 100 Americans helped to persuade America to join the war.

Right. A German U-boat of 1916. Diesel engines charged the batteries for underwater motion and propelled the vessel on the surface.

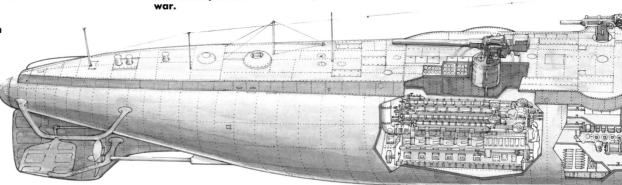

22

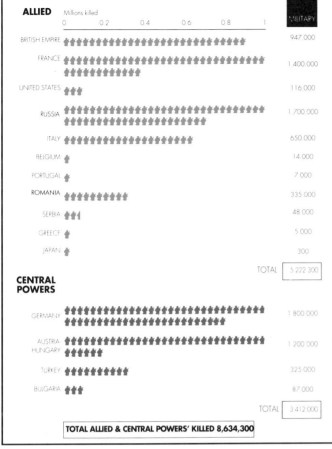

ALLIED	Millions killed					MILITARY
	0	0.2	0.4	0.6	0.8	1
BRITISH EMPIRE						947,000
FRANCE						1,400,000
UNITED STATES						116,000
RUSSIA						1,700,000
ITALY						650,000
BELGIUM						14,000
PORTUGAL						7,000
ROMANIA						335,000
SERBIA						48,000
GREECE						5,000
JAPAN						300
					TOTAL	5,222,300
CENTRAL POWERS						
GERMANY						1,800,000
AUSTRIA HUNGARY						1,200,000
TURKEY						325,000
BULGARIA						87,000
					TOTAL	3,412,000

TOTAL ALLIED & CENTRAL POWERS' KILLED 8,634,300

Civilian Casualties

The First World War was the first war to involve large numbers of civilian casualties. The Germans brought war to the British people through naval bombardments of the coastal towns of Scunthorpe and Scarborough. At first, air raids were carried out by giant airships, Zeppelins, but after several of these were shot down, the Germans used airplanes. Altogether, just over 1,100 civilians were killed in Britain because of the war.

In France and Belgium the civilians were much worse off. As the Germans invaded France in 1914 much of the two countries was overrun and many civilians lost their homes, and some their lives, as the two armies battled for advances. Some small towns were completely destroyed by shelling from either side.

also failing to produce food, because so many men had gone to fight that there were not enough left to work on the farms. When Germany began to lose more and more battles, its leaders were afraid that shortages at home would lead to a revolution.

The Easter Rising

One unexpected result of the war was an attempt by sections of the Irish volunteer army and nationalist sympathizers to set up an Irish Republic.

On Easter Monday in 1916, seven men set up a headquarters at the central post office in Dublin and proclaimed a republic. After five days of fighting, British troops regained control of the city. The men who had signed the proclamation were shot. Others were charged with treason and sentenced to be hanged. One of the army leaders who escaped the death penalty was Eamon De Valera, later to become the Republic's first president.

Above. World leaders — American president Woodrow Wilson, center, signed the Treaty of Versailles in 1919 with French prime minister Clemenceau, left, and British prime minister Lloyd George, right.

GERMANY IS DEFEATED Russia left the war after signing the Treaty of Brest-Litovsk on March 3, 1918. Germany was now free to concentrate on the Western Front and made one last effort to defeat the Allies.

In March, a massive German attack broke through the French and British lines on the Somme. Led by Field Marshal Foch, the Allied armies, including a US army under General Pershing, fought back. The Germans soon ran out of supplies and by the end of April their advance halted. Now Allied forces attacked at the Battle of the Marne and Allied tanks advanced towards Germany.

During the final days of the war the old Austro-Hungarian Empire collapsed, as its individual states declared independence and made peace with the Allies.

On November 9, the German Kaiser was forced to resign and a new republican government took over. Germany signed an *armistice*, a cease-fire, with the Allies on November 11. War was at an end.

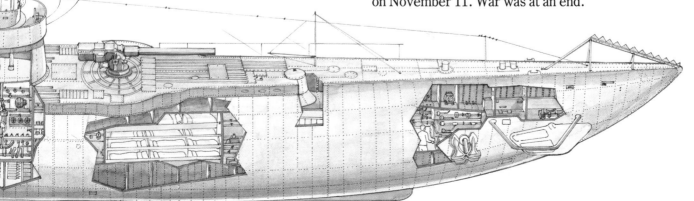

Political Changes

THE RUSSIAN REVOLUTION

St. Petersburg in 1917. Violence breaks out as revolutionaries take to the streets to fight for a Communist government.

Russia suffered huge losses during the First World War (see pages 20–21) and its civilian population was starving. Tsar Nicholas II was forced to abdicate in March 1917 and was succeeded by a republican government, led by Prince Lvov, which did not last long. In July, a lawyer named Alexander Kerensky became prime minister, but his government was divided and deeply unpopular.

FALL OF THE GOVERNMENT A number of small but influential Marxist groups led the opposition to Kerensky's government. The most important of these was the *Bolsheviks*, led by Vladimir Ilyich Ulyanov, who was better known as Lenin.

The war was going badly and many Russian soldiers had begun to mutiny. Kerensky had given guns to the committees of workers, called *soviets*, whom he hoped would remain loyal to him. In fact, many members of the soviets were Bolsheviks, loyal to Lenin.

Lenin and Trotsky

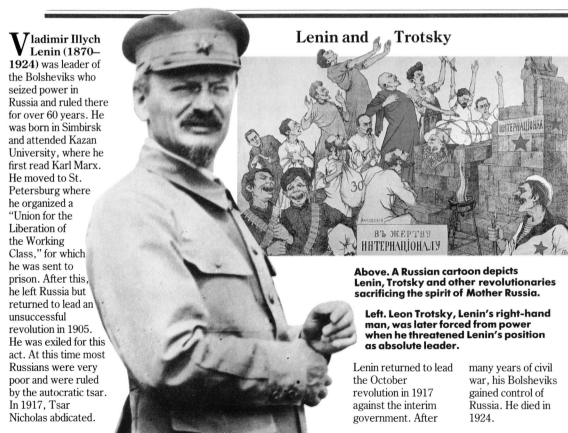

Vladimir Illych Lenin (1870–1924) was leader of the Bolsheviks who seized power in Russia and ruled there for over 60 years. He was born in Simbirsk and attended Kazan University, where he first read Karl Marx. He moved to St. Petersburg where he organized a "Union for the Liberation of the Working Class," for which he was sent to prison. After this, he left Russia but returned to lead an unsuccessful revolution in 1905. He was exiled for this act. At this time most Russians were very poor and were ruled by the autocratic tsar. In 1917, Tsar Nicholas abdicated.

Above. A Russian cartoon depicts Lenin, Trotsky and other revolutionaries sacrificing the spirit of Mother Russia.

Left. Leon Trotsky, Lenin's right-hand man, was later forced from power when he threatened Lenin's position as absolute leader.

Lenin returned to lead the October revolution in 1917 against the interim government. After many years of civil war, his Bolsheviks gained control of Russia. He died in 1924.

Leon Trotsky (1879–1940) As a young man, Trotsky was imprisoned for agitating, but he escaped and fled to London where he met Lenin. He was involved in the unsuccessful 1905 coup and was again imprisoned. He escaped, then returned to Russia in 1917 to help lead the revolution. After this he built up and led the Red Army to victory in the civil war against the White Russians. He was opposed to Lenin's successor, Stalin, was expelled from the Communist Party and was killed in Mexico by one of Stalin's assassins.

Supported by factions from different revolutionary groups, including the *Menshevik* or "minority" Marxist groups, Lenin called upon Kerensky's government to surrender. Early in the morning of November 7, 1917, groups of revolutionaries, armed with guns and supported by units of the Russian army, advanced upon the Winter Palace in Petrograd (St. Petersburg) where the government was based. The ship *Aurora*, which was anchored in the River Neva, fired a few shots at the palace. There was no opposition and in a short while the government had fallen.

Joseph Stalin ruled the USSR with a rod of iron from 1924–1953.

Communists took control of industry, banks and transport, and confiscated the land and property of the Russian Orthodox Church.

In March 1918, Lenin's government signed the Treaty of Brest-Litovsk with Germany, withdrawing from the war and allowing Germany to keep the parts of Ukraine that it had taken over.

CIVIL WAR IN RUSSIA Any hopes that the tsar would return faded in July 1918, when the Communists ordered the execution of Nicholas II and all his family. Even so, there was civil war in Russia from 1918 to 1922, as supporters of the monarchy (helped by Britain and France) attempted to overthrow the Communist government. It was a time of great bloodshed and hardship.

LENIN'S COMMUNIST GOVERNMENT Lenin's Bolsheviks quickly established themselves as the main group in the revolutionary government, keeping the more moderate Mensheviks out of positions of power. The Bolsheviks renamed themselves "Communists," a name taken from Marx and Engels's *Communist Manifesto* of 1848.

The new government passed laws giving peasants the right to seize land held by the aristocracy. The

THE RISE OF STALIN By the time Lenin died in January 1924, he was firmly in control of the new Communist state. After his death, power passed into the hands of one of his party officials, Joseph Stalin. The new leader was not interested in communism's original ideas about justice and fairness and he became a ruthless tyrant.

War in Russia 1918–1921

Left. A Russian poster calls for opposition to world fascism. It is easy to forget that Russia, more than any other nation, helped to defeat Hitler's Germany.

Above. Nations such as Britain, America, France and Germany aided and encouraged counter-revolutionary forces to fight a civil war against Russia's Bolsheviks.

Russian losses 1918

White resistance overcome

→ Intervention repulsed

SOCIAL REFORM

The Russian revolution (see pages 24–25) provided the world with an example of a state looking after the needs and well-being of all its citizens. Western governments took many years to grant their citizens similar rights. They finally did so because of pressure for reform from workers' organizations and other groups.

In the early years of the century, few countries had *pensions* for old people, or paid *benefits* to those who were unemployed or too sick to work. New Zealand was the only country where women could vote. In some countries, people were not allowed to form *trade unions*.

SOCIALISM Communism (revolutionary socialism) was unpopular in Europe. But democratic socialism aimed to bring about social changes through laws passed in Parliament. In Britain, these Socialists were represented by the Labour Party. The first Labour government was elected in 1924 and was led by Ramsay MacDonald. This government lasted less than a year, but the Socialist movement remained important.

The success of this movement was at first due to its close links with trades unions, who used their money to support the election of members of Parliament who agreed with their ideas. Before World War I, trade unions became very powerful in Britain, France, Germany and the US. They went on strike to force governments to agree to social reforms, and to gain political power for working people.

ELECTORAL REFORM The slogan, "votes for women," was heard more and more in the early 1900s. Women who campaigned for the vote were called "suffragettes," because they wanted "suffrage" (the right to vote). In Britain, their leaders were Emmeline Pankhurst and her daughter Christabel. The suffragettes drew attention to their cause through actions such as hunger strikes and chaining themselves to the railings of government offices. Many were imprisoned.

At the end of World War I, the vote was given to women in Britian who were over 30 years of age and were married to householders. But in 1928, with the support of the Labour Party, women were given the vote on the same terms as men. Many other countries were slower to change.

THE WELFARE STATE A *welfare state* is a country which provides money and support to the old, sick, unemployed and so on.

In Britain, the Liberal government of 1906 made the first moves towards this. It introduced small pensions for people over 70 years of age, and a *national insurance* scheme, covering sickness and unemployment, to which employers, employees and the state all contributed.

In 1942 the British economist, Sir William Beveridge, first used the term "welfare state" and said that the state should look after its citizens *from the cradle to the grave.*" The Labour government that came to power after World War II put his ideas into practice, and by 1948 Britain had a National Health Service which gave free treatment to everyone. The government also paid cash allowances to mothers to help them bring up their children; improved pensions, unemployment benefits and sick pay.

Social change was slower to begin in the US. State pensions were not introduced until the early 1920s. Improvements to conditions of employment came with the Social Security Act of 1935, which increased old age pensions and introduced unemployment benefits, and help for poor children.

During the depression of the 1930s, many working-class families lived in cramped slum conditions. Many suffered ill-health as a result and the infant mortality rate was high.

Child mineworkers in the US. In the early years of the century most American states had no laws to prevent child labor.

1 In the US President Franklin D. Roosevelt introduces his **New Deal.** This was legislation set up to help the American economy to recover from the depression of the thirties. Laws were passed to make farmers produce the right crops, and to give the president powers to oversee many banking and financial deals. Money was also made available to invest in the economy where needed and new taxes were raised.

2 British power in India began to decline from about 1920 onwards. In 1919, 379 Indians were shot dead and over 1,000 injured when British troops fired on a crowd in Amritsar. Mohandas Gandhi called for a non-violent protest against British rule and a boycott of all foreign goods. His following grew and many workers went on strike in protest against British rule. Gandhi's peaceful protest led in 1947 to Indian Independence.

Political Change

In Britain, poor working conditions brought about a general strike in which over three million workers from all industries brought the nation to a standstill for nine days in 1926. Miners whose claim for a living wage had sparked off the strike were defeated and they had no choice but to return to work after six months of near starvation.

But the inter-war years were also years of important political change. War had made people challenge the established political parties and look for new solutions. Britain's first Labour government was elected in 1924 and the general election of 1929 was the first in which all women were allowed to vote.

Suffragettes who were imprisoned often went on hunger strikes and were brutally force fed by prison doctors.

TREATMENT OF POLITICAL PRISONERS UNDER A LIBERAL GOVERNMENT.

When Women Got the Vote

One of the most striking features of the 20th century has been the increased part that women play in society. In Britain, until the middle of the last century, they had no right to vote, to enter universities or the professions, or to own property. They could not keep their earnings, or even their children if their husband chose to leave or divorce them. By 1914, some of these wrongs had been corrected but people's attitudes were hard to change.

Two world wars, education and full employment have brought enormous changes in attitudes towards women's rights and such questions as divorce, equal pay and careers for married women. Even so, some people feel that women are still badly off, and that much remains to be done before people recognize that men and women are truly equal.

New Zealand	1893
Australia	1902
Denmark	1915
USSR	1917
Austria	1918
Germany	1918
Britain	1919
Belgium	1919
Ireland	1919
US	1920
India	1926
Pakistan	1926
France	1944
Italy	1945
Japan	1945
Israel	1948
Indonesia	1955
Switzerland	1971
Jordan	1973

Women still do not have the vote in many, mainly Moslem, countries, including Iran, Iraq, United Arab Emirates, Saudi Arabia and Kuwait.

DEPRESSION AND DICTATORSHIPS

$100 WILL BUY THIS CAR MUST HAVE CASH LOST ALL ON THE STOCK MARKET

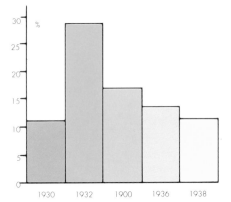

Left. A New York stockbroker is forced to sell his car as billions of dollars are wiped off the value of shares in one day.

Above. Industrial output fell to a record low in 1930.

Right. World unemployment reached a peak of almost 30 percent in the early 1930s.

The countries that had fought in the First World War were slow to recover. The high number of casualties in the armed forces meant that nations such as France, Germany, Russia and Britain had lost a generation of young men. Industries which had been producing weapons found it difficult to adapt to the needs of peacetime. There was no money to invest in new machinery, so factories used old working methods that were expensive and inefficient. Soldiers everywhere returned home to unemployment, poor housing, low wages and little hope for the future.

DEPRESSION In October 1929, a world wide *recession*, very bad economic conditions, set in. In the United States, eight or nine million workers lost their jobs. There was little or no government help for them. The number of people out of work in Germany rose to six million. This period is known as the Great Depression.

THE NEW DICTATORSHIPS In many countries, people looked for extreme solutions to their economic and political problems. Dictators, rulers with absolute power, took control in some countries. The first was Benito

Mussolini, who came to power in Italy in October 1922.

People said of Mussolini that "*he made the trains run on time.*" Il Duce, as he was called, gained popular support because of his major building projects. These provided jobs at a time of unemployment, created a modern transport system, and helped Italian industry to recover. Adolf Hitler (see pages 30–31), who came to power in Germany in 1935, adopted many of Mussolini's strategies to end unemployment and help industry.

World War I had been called "a war to end wars," and after it was over the Allies had set up the League of Nations, where politicians could discuss their problems instead of going to war. However, during the 1930s acts of war increased.

Italy invaded Abyssinia (Ethiopia) in 1935, using planes and modern weapons against the poorly equipped Abyssinian troops. The countries of the League of Nations reduced trade with Italy as a punishment, but this did not stop Italy from adding the independent African state to its small overseas empire.

In 1936 civil war broke out in Spain between the republican government and right-wing forces led by General Franco. Britain gave financial aid to Franco and

Right. In Spain, the artist Pablo Picasso captures the world's horror at the killing of innocent civilians in an air raid on the town of Guernica during the Spanish civil war.

Below. General Franco led a fascist revolt against the legitimate left-wing republican government. Franco took over as a dictator in 1939 and ruled until his death in 1975.

Prohibition

On October 28, 1920, the National Prohibition Act became law in the US. Its aim was to prohibit the manufacture, distribution and sale of alcohol, and it was passed because drunkenness was a widespread social problem among the working classes. A strong religious lobby thought alcohol was evil and should be banned.

Instead of making America a safer place to live, the Prohibition laws actually led to violent gang warfare as rival interests, including the Mafia, sought to gain control of the lucrative but illegal business of distilling and selling alcohol.

The government finally realized that the Prohibition laws could not be enforced and they were repealed in 1933.

Italian East Africa 1935

The invasion and dividing-up of the Horn of Africa proved more difficult than the European invaders expected. The Italians colonized Eritrea to the north and Italian Somaliland to the east.

Italian conquests 1935–1936

In Italy, Benito Mussolini, Il Duce, rekindled his country's pride through a military-style dictatorship. He provided jobs in a time of high unemployment by starting major building projects. Mussolini came to power in October 1922 following his "March on Rome" – an armed demonstration that forced Italy's King Victor Emmanuel III to grant him absolute power.

Germany lent him tanks, planes and pilots, which helped to give him victory three years later.

THE OLD WORLD POWERS During the 1920s and 1930s, Britain and the US paid little attention to the increasing signs of aggression from the new rising powers within Europe and the Far East.

Meanwhile, the Soviet Union under Stalin (see p. 25) was trying to become an industrial power to compete with the countries of western Europe and North America. Stalin forced small landowners to give up their farms so that they could be joined together to make large *collectivized* farms. New farming methods could then be used to make these farms more productive. Reforms were forced upon the Soviet people and anyone who resisted Stalin was executed or sent into exile in Siberia. During the same period, China suffered a long civil war, in which Chiang Kai-shek's government troops fought with Communist forces.

29

THE RISE OF ADOLF HITLER

The Great Depression that hit all of the Western world in the 1920s and early 1930s was even worse in Germany, because it was paying off heavy debts after World War I. Prices rose so fast that banknotes became almost worthless. The German people were desperate for a solution to their problems.

THE NAZI PARTY The National Socialist, or Nazi, Party led by Adolf Hitler was rapidly gaining popularity. Hitler blamed low wages and high unemployment on the Jewish businesses in Germany. He organized a small private army called the SA, or *Sturm Abteilungen*. Dressed in their brown shirts and jack boots, the SA acted as guards at Nazi rallies and beat up Communists and Jews.

In 1925, Hitler used the SA to try to overthrow the state government of Bavaria and seize power. The attempt failed and he was jailed for three years, during which time he wrote a book about his political ideas. It was called *Mein Kampf*, "My Struggle," and it became a bestseller. Because Hitler was violently opposed to communism, he was able to make an alliance with the weak Catholic Center Party. After the 1932 elections, the Nazis and the Center Party formed a government. Hitler was made chancellor, or prime minister.

THE NAZIS SEIZE POWER In 1933 the German parliament building, the Reichstag, was burnt to the ground, probably by the SA. Hitler said that it was a Communist plot, using this as an excuse to extend his powers and end democracy in Germany.

Left. Adolf Hitler addresses his massed armies at Nuremburg in 1938. In less than a year he was to take his country to war.

Germany after World War I

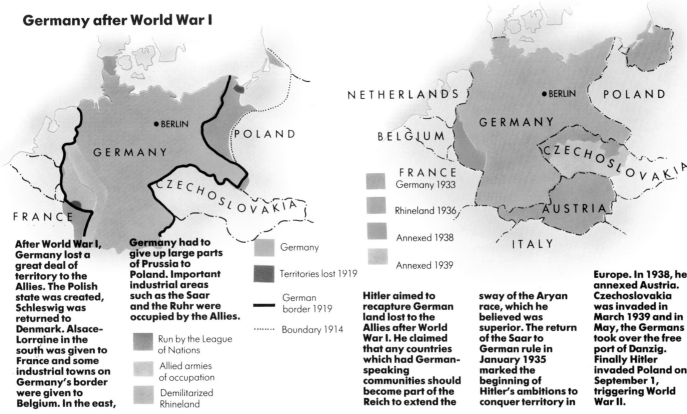

After World War I, Germany lost a great deal of territory to the Allies. The Polish state was created, Schleswig was returned to Denmark. Alsace-Lorraine in the south was given to France and some industrial towns on Germany's border were given to Belgium. In the east,

Germany had to give up large parts of Prussia to Poland. Important industrial areas such as the Saar and the Ruhr were occupied by the Allies.

Germany

Territories lost 1919

German border 1919

Boundary 1914

Run by the League of Nations

Allied armies of occupation

Demilitarized Rhineland

Germany 1933

Rhineland 1936

Annexed 1938

Annexed 1939

Hitler aimed to recapture German land lost to the Allies after World War I. He claimed that any countries which had German-speaking communities should become part of the Reich to extend the

sway of the Aryan race, which he believed was superior. The return of the Saar to German rule in January 1935 marked the beginning of Hitler's ambitions to conquer territory in

Europe. In 1938, he annexed Austria. Czechoslovakia was invaded in March 1939 and in May, the Germans took over the free port of Danzig. Finally Hitler invaded Poland on September 1, triggering World War II.

But Hitler could not be sure of total power while the SA was strong enough to stage a *coup* and overthrow him. On June 30, 1934, "Night of the Long Knives," Hitler ordered loyal Nazis to assassinate key members of the SA. Hundreds of SA troopers were killed.

GERMANY PREPARES FOR WAR Hitler then set about building up his armed forces, buying weapons and introducing conscription so that all young men spent a certain amount of time in the armed forces. He wanted to recover the lands that Germany had been forced to give up after the 1914–1918 war. In 1935, Germany regained the Saar area from the French. A year later, German forces re-occupied the Rhineland.

In 1938, Hitler sent tanks into Vienna and forced Austria to agree to be united with Germany. In that same year he said he would take over the Sudetenland, the part of Czechoslovakia that bordered Germany, where about three million German-speaking people lived. The leaders of France, Britain and Italy agreed not to prevent a Germany invasion of Czechoslovakia. Hitler believed he could not be stopped in his ambition to expand Germany. He now turned his attention to Poland, which in 1919 had been granted a strip of land that gave it access to the port

of Danzig. Called the Polish corridor, this strip of land divided the German state of Prussia into two. Hitler demanded that Danzig be handed over to Germany, together with the right to travel through the Polish corridor. Poland refused, and Britain and France guaranteed their support if Germany attacked.

On September 1, 1939, German troops poured into Poland, and as a result Britain and France declared war on Germany.

Left. Runaway inflation meant that banknotes lost their value almost as soon as they were printed.

Above. Hitler's brownshirts forced Jews to perform menial tasks, such as cleaning the streets by hand.

THE DOMINATION OF EUROPE

World War II was sparked off by Germany's invasion of Poland. But, although they declared war on Germany, there was nothing Britain and France could do to help the Poles.

Germany's armies used new tactics called *blitzkrieg*, lightning war. First, they sent in dive-bombers to do as much damage as possible. Then they attacked by land, using tanks followed by infantry. An hour after the German invasion of Poland, the city of Warsaw had been bombed and half the Polish air force had been destroyed before it had even taken off. Within a month, Germany had taken over Poland.

THE 'PHONEY WAR' British troops were sent to France to help fight against the expected German attack. But nothing happened immediately. This period is often called the "phoney war." People wondered what was going to happen. In Britain, civilians were given gas masks and children were sent from the towns to the countryside in case of a surprise bomb attack.

Then, in April 1940, Germany invaded neutral Norway and Denmark. This was to stop Britain's navy from attacking the supplies of iron ore that Germany obtained from Sweden.

GERMANY ON THE ATTACK After World War I, France had built a heavily fortified wall along its border with Germany, in case of attack. This wall was known as the Maginot Line. However, in May 1940 German panzer, or tank, divisions rolled through Belgium and the Netherlands, so bypassing the Maginot Line. British and French troops moved north into Belgium to fight, but were surrounded by German panzer forces which had moved through the Ardennes forest.

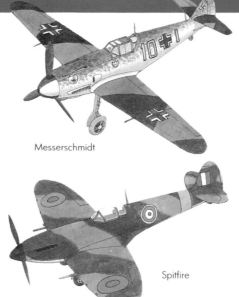

Messerschmidt

Spitfire

The Spitfire

The Supermarine Spitfire (pictured below), designed by Reginald Joseph Mitchell, and the Hawker Hurricane enabled a small number of British pilots to gain control of the skies from the many German bombers and fighters, including the Messerschmidt 109, sent to destroy them.

The British and French retreated towards the coast and escaped from Dunkirk to Britain.

After this, Field Marshall Pétain, the leader of France, signed a cease-fire agreement with Germany. France was divided in two. The northern zone was under German military rule and the southern zone was governed by a French government set up at Vichy but controlled by Germany.

BRITAIN STANDS ALONE Britain became the center of resistance to Hitler's Germany. Members of European

EIRE GREAT BRITAIN
PORTUGAL
SPAIN
FRANCE
SWITZERLAND
NORWAY SWEDEN FINLAND
SOVIET RUSSIA
GERMANY POLAND CZECHOSLOVAKIA HUNGARY ROMANIA
AUSTRIA
ITALY BULGARIA
BLACK SEA
TURKEY
MEDITERRANEAN
TUNISIA
LIBYA EGYPT

Europe under Hitler 1942

The map shows the extent of German occupied territory in Europe 1939–1945. Hitler had expanded | **his empire to its greatest extent right across Europe in November 1942.**

☐ Axis and satellite territories

☐ Axis occupied territories

☐ Opponents of the Axis Powers

☐ Neutral countries

The Ghetto

Warsaw, the capital of Poland, was almost completely destroyed by the German army during World War II. The Germans surrounded the city in 1939 and it was badly damaged in the siege. The German troops terrorized the people of Warsaw. They arrested thousands and killed many without trial. They put about 500,000 Jews in a small area called the ghetto. Many died from disease or were killed by the Germans.

governments who had fled from their own countries to Britain encouraged their citizens to help defeat Nazism. People who had managed to escape from occupied France and Poland fought alongside the British forces.

Britain itself was attacked, too. Between August 15 and September 15, 1940, German bombers raided British cities and airfields as the first stage in a planned invasion. These air attacks were known as the Battle of Britain and they ended in victory for the Royal Air Force (RAF). Although the German planes outnumbered the British by two to one, they lost almost twice as many aircraft as the British. Finally their losses forced them to abandon these major bombing raids.

The RAF owed its success partly to the fast and maneuverable Spitfire airplane. The pilots who fought in the Battle of Britain were known as the "Few." Many of them were killed.

At sea, British and neutral merchant ships came under increasing attack from the German submarines, the U-boats. For a long time it looked as if Germany would succeed in cutting the vital supplies of food and raw materials imported into Britain from overseas.

German bombs destroyed most of London's center and East End but St. Paul's Cathedral escaped destruction.

The Germans overran Europe with *blitzkrieg*, lightning war, tactics. Rapidly advancing tanks broke down enemy resistance while infantry followed quickly behind. In this way the German army quickly overran Poland. Following **the invasion of Denmark and Norway, German armies overran the Netherlands, Belgium and Luxembourg in May 1940. In the following month the defeat of the French army gave Hitler control of most of western Europe.**

THE WORLD AT WAR

Above. US Marines come ashore during the Pacific war.

Right. This Russian cartoon shows how the Allies would defeat Hitler by fighting Germany on all fronts.

THE NORTH AFRICA CAMPAIGN

Italy joined the war as Germany's ally on July 10, 1940. The alliance was called the Axis. Italy's dictator, Mussolini, was keen to share in Germany's victories.

In September 1940, Italian forces entered Egypt, where the British had a small army protecting the Suez Canal, which was a vital link between Britain and its empire. The British army soon pushed the poorly trained and badly equipped Italians back into Libya, taking thousands of prisoners.

Hitler sent troops and tanks, commanded by General Rommel, to fight in North Africa. For the next two years British and Axis forces fought for control of the area. General Montgomery's Eighth Army finally defeated Rommel's Afrika Corps at El Alamein in Egypt in October 1942.

By the end of that year, the British had defeated the Italian navy, which allowed them to cut off German supplies to North Africa. Allied forces landed in Algeria and Morocco and linked up with Montgomery's forces. The Axis forces in North Africa surrendered in the following May.

B y the end of 1940, Hitler thought that Britain was no longer a threat to his ambitions. He turned his attention to the Soviet Union.

Besides hating communism, Hitler believed that the Slavs and Russians were inferior to German people. He wanted to take their territory and turn them into slaves to work for the expansion of Germany.

OPERATION BARBAROSSA In 1939, Germany and the Soviet Union had made an agreement not to fight each other, but in June 1941 Hitler turned his back on this agreement and launched Operation Barbarossa: the invasion of the Soviet Union.

Hitler started his campaign hoping for a quick victory. But even though the German army was much better organized and better equipped than the Soviets', the invasion used up valuable German resources and caused heavy casualties. It was on the battlefields of Russia that Germany began to lose the war.

Right. The Allies' main tank in the last part of the war was the American-built Sherman.

AMERICA ENTERS THE WAR After the Japanese attack on the US Pacific fleet at Pearl Harbor (see page 39), Germany, which was Japan's ally, declared war on the US on December 11, 1941. Three world powers – Britain, the Soviet Union and the US – were now ranged against Germany. But it was not easy to defeat Germany. The US had to fight in the east as well as in Europe. Britain and the US also had to send supplies to the Soviets to help them fight Germany.

By the end of 1941 the Germans had got within sight of Moscow.

34

Left. Operation Overlord was launched against beaches in Normandy.

FRANCE

Ships assembled here

→ Invasion routes

The War in Europe 1942–1945

Left. The Allied offensive in Europe began with the invasion of Italy and the landings in northern France. To the east the Russians broke through the German lines in Poland in January 1945. On March 7 the Allied armies crossed the river Rhine into Germany, and on May 1 as Soviet forces entered the city of Berlin, Hitler and his wife Eva Braun committed suicide in his bunker.

MURMANSK

FINLAND

NORWAY

SWEDEN

DENMARK

LENINGRAD

USSR

KONIGSBERG

MOSCOW

GREAT BRITAIN

LONDON

MINSK

KURSK

WARSAW

ARDENNES

BERLIN

CAEN

PARIS

PRAGUE

KIEV

STALINGRAD

GERMANY

FRANCE

ITALY

BUDAPEST

ISTANBUL

ROME

ANZIO

CASSINO

TURKEY

TRIPOLI

EL ALAMEIN

Right. Infantry uniforms of World War II. From left to right, the United States of America, Germany, Britain, Italy and Russia. Many soldiers who had escaped from their own countries, such as Poles, fought in special units with the Allied forces.

→ Allied advances

→ German movements

⇢ German counter-attacks

✷ Major battles

35

One of the most savage air raids of the war. In a single night, Dresden was virtually flattened by Allied bombing.

After the Axis forces in North Africa surrendered in May 1943, the way was clear for the Allies to push into Italy and begin to fight the Germans and Italians in a different area. This was the second front that Stalin had been asking for (see p. 34).

THE ALLIES LAND IN ITALY The invasion of the island of Sicily began in July and the Axis forces did not do much to resist it. Mussolini's close advisers told him to resign. A new Italian government approached the Allies to ask for peace.

Allied forces moved to the mainland of Italy and began a rapid advance. By the beginning of 1944, they had reached Rome. But their advance was slowed down by a German army which was determined to hold on to northern Italy. Mussolini was still the ruler there, although he was now controlled by the Germans.

DEFEAT IN RUSSIA After the German forces were pushed back from Moscow at the end of 1941 (see page 34), Hitler moved his armies south to capture the oil fields of the Caucasus. By the autumn of 1942, he had decided to take the city of Stalingrad.

The Germans besieged the city and bombarded it with *artillery*, heavy field guns. Although they were outnumbered by three to one, the Soviet forces held on to the city, fighting ferociously. In late November, more Soviet troops arrived to relieve the city. It was the Germans' turn to be surrounded. In an attack that lasted

ALLIED (Millions killed)	Military killed	Civilian killed
BRITISH EMPIRE COMMONWEALTH	452,000	60,000
FRANCE	250,000	360,000
UNITED STATES	295,000	
RUSSIA	13,600,000	7,700,000
BELGIUM	10,000	90,000
HOLLAND	10,000	190,000
NORWAY	10,000	
POLAND	120,000	5,300,000
GREECE	20,000	80,000
YUGOSLAVIA	300,000	1,300,000
CZECHOSLOVAKIA	20,000	330,000
CHINA	3,500,000	10,000,000
TOTAL ALLIED MILITARY & CIVILIAN KILLED 43,997,000	18,587,000	25,410,000
AXIS		
GERMANY	3,250,000	3,810,000
AUSTRIA	230,000	80,000
ITALY	330,000	85,000
ROMANIA	200,000	465,000
HUNGARY	120,000	280,000
BULGARIA	10,000	7,000
FINLAND	90,000	
JAPAN	1,700,000	360,000
TOTAL AXIS MILITARY & CIVILIAN KILLED 11,017,000	18,587,000	25,410,000

Including Jewish deaths

TOTAL ALLIED KILLED & AXIS KILLED 55,014,000

Russia suffered by far the highest casualty rate of any country fighting in World War II, both in military and civilian terms. Poland lost a great number of civilians.

from 10 January to 2 February 1943 Soviet troops killed 100,000 German soldiers and took a further 110,000 prisoner. Of those taken prisoner, most died because of the harsh conditions in which they were kept.

The following year the Soviets defeated a major German attack. For the first time in the war they also

The Holocaust

Hitler wanted to create a strong German master race of fair-haired blue-eyed "Aryans," so he set about eliminating people he thought were racially inferior, like the Jews and the gypsies, and also the disabled and mentally handicapped.

But it was the Jews who attracted his particular hatred. Like many other Germans, he resented Jewish businessmen whom he thought were conspiring to rob German people of money and jobs. Hitler planned to kill all the Jews in Europe, in what he called the "final solution to the Jewish question."

Prisoners in a concentration camp cheer the soldiers freeing them.

The Germans hated the Jews so much that when Hitler started persecuting them, hardly anyone protested at the terrible cruelty and injustice. First, he took away their rights as citizens. Then he made them live in separate areas called ghettoes. Finally, he began a deliberate program to exterminate the Jews by taking them away to special concentration camps in eastern Europe, where they were kept in the most dreadful conditions then gassed, shot, tortured or starved to death.

By the end of the war in 1945, Hitler's SS had murdered around six million innocent Jews.

The Attempt to Kill Hitler

On the morning of July 20, 1944, a German officer planted a bomb hidden in a briefcase under the table where Hitler and his generals were planning their military campaign. Minutes later there was an enormous explosion.

Thinking Hitler had been killed, Colonel Claus von Stauffenburg telephoned his fellow conspirators in Berlin.

But the table had turned away the full force of the blast and Hitler was only slightly injured. The conspirators were quickly arrested and some of them, including von Stauffenburg, were shot.

The Italian Campaign 1943–1945

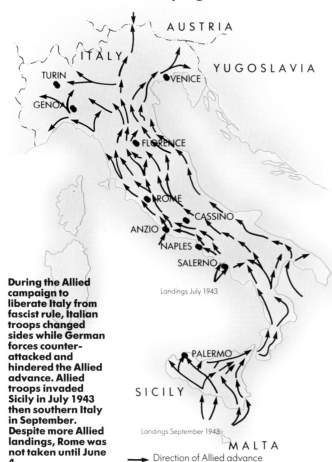

During the Allied campaign to liberate Italy from fascist rule, Italian troops changed sides while German forces counter-attacked and hindered the Allied advance. Allied troops invaded Sicily in July 1943 then southern Italy in September. Despite more Allied landings, Rome was not taken until June 4.

Landings July 1943

Landings September 1943

→ Direction of Allied advance

launched an attack first, forcing the Germans to withdraw.

Supplies were now getting through to the Soviet army, partly because of Allied aid and partly because of great increases in industrial production. The Red Army began a march westwards that only ended when they reached Berlin, the German capital.

OPERATION OVERLORD Just before dawn on June 6, 1944, the Allies landed on five beaches in Normandy, northern France. They had previously spread false information about what they were going to do, so the Germans were expecting them to land further to the east. The first troops ashore soon won through. By the end of the day, 156,000 men had landed in Normandy. More and more Allied troops poured into Europe, forcing the German army to withdraw.

Although the Germans were now certain to be defeated, Hitler launched a campaign of bomb and rocket attacks on Britain. In reply, the Allies stepped up their bombing raids on German cities like Hamburg and Dresden, hoping to end the war more quickly.

On April 23, 1945, Mussolini was captured and shot by Italians who were opposed to his rule. Shortly afterwards the German forces in Italy surrendered. On April 30, 1945, with Soviet troops already entering Berlin, Adolf Hitler shot himself. Eight days later, his successor, Admiral Doenitz, surrendered to the Allies. The war in Europe was over.

THE RISING SUN

The War in the East

CHINA

PACIFIC OCEAN

JAPAN

BURMA

PHILIPPINES

DUTCH EAST INDIES

NEW GUINEA

AUSTRALIA

NEW ZEALAND

Japan

Area of Japanese conquest

Above. The extent of Japan's conquests. Most of the territory was taken in just six months of fighting. From 1943 their overstretched forces were forced to retreat.

Above. US warships are sunk at Pearl Harbor in a surprise attack that signaled the outbreak of war with Japan.
Right. Japanese suicide pilots sacrificed their lives to defend their country.

In the years between the two world wars, Japan rose from a backward feudal nation to become an industrialized world power with a fast-growing population. Yet Japan's system of government was old-fashioned and undemocratic, headed by an emperor who was regarded as a god.

THE ARMY TAKES CONTROL In 1936, army officers took control of the government, with the approval of the emperor. During the late 1930s, Japan took advantage of the civil war in China (see page 29), conquering large sections of that country. Japanese troops treated the Chinese brutally, killing 250,000 civilians in the city of Nanjing alone.

When war broke out in Europe, Japan realized that a weakened British Empire would be unable to prevent it

from extending its influence in the Far East and the Pacific.

The United States of America responded to Japanese attempts of expansion by announcing that it would not export any more oil to Japan until the Japanese withdrew all their troops from China. Discussions between the two countries failed to reach an agreement on this issue, and Japan began to consider a military solution to its problems.

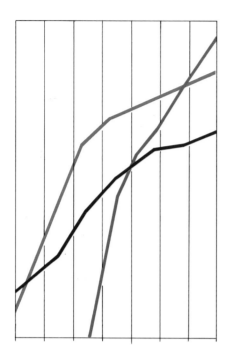

Japanese Industry

Today, manufacturing industry is the most important area of work in Japan. At the turn of the century, the Japanese were not able to produce large amounts of steel, a vital part of building up their country. Between 1900 and 1940 the output of steel rose 1000%, helping to build railways which covered more of the country every year.

Right. The American B-29 Superfortress with the atomic bombs used against Japan. In the last stages of the war, waves of bombers rained destruction on Japan's industrial cities.

Below. The first atomic bomb destroyed the city of Hiroshima on August 6, 1945.

Rebuilding Japan

The post-war recovery of Japan was extremely slow but it was helped by an American aid program. Japan was eventually allowed to rebuild her large industrial companies which had been disbanded after the war. From about 1947 onwards Japan was allowed a limited amount of international trade. Under the terms of her surrender Japan was not allowed to keep an army – and this condition remains unaltered today. Because it keeps no army, Japan has not had to spend money on defense. This has left the country free to invest more money in rebuilding its industry and infrastructure. Japan's disadvantages eventually became its advantages.

PEARL HARBOR On December 7, 1941, Japan launched a surprise bombing raid on Pearl Harbor in Hawaii, sinking almost the entire US Pacific fleet. The following day, the United States and Britain declared war on Japan. Shortly afterwards, Germany and Italy, which were Japan's allies, declared war on the US.

Japanese forces surprised the Allies by moving swiftly to capture Hong Kong. The following February, the British troops in Singapore surrendered to a Japanese army which had attacked after traveling through jungle that the British had thought no one could get through.

Within six months the Japanese had conquered the Dutch East Indies, Burma, the Philippines and the islands of the South Pacific. But in June 1942 the American fleet won a decisive victory at the Battle of Midway, sinking Japan's four largest aircraft carriers.

From mid-1943 onward, Japan's army, which was stretched over too wide an area, began to suffer defeat in the US attacks upon the Pacific islands and the British campaign in the jungle of Burma. To the Japanese, defeat meant dishonor. They would rather die than surrender. This opinion meant that they thought anyone else who surrendered had acted dishonorably. Japanese soldiers treated captured Allied soldiers like slaves and forced them to work on projects such as the Burma railway, where many died of heat, disease and hunger.

DEFEAT OF JAPAN By 1944, the Allies were able to blockade Japan, preventing ships from going in or out of Japanese ports. This meant that Japan could not obtain iron or steel, rubber or oil. As they captured more Pacific islands from the Japanese, the US Air Force used them to launch bombing raids on Japanese cities.

The US Navy and Army advanced towards Japan and fighting became more intense. With just enough fuel left to fly their planes, the Japanese *kamikaze* pilots flew suicide missions against US warships.

Japan still refused to surrender. On August 6, 1945, a US plane dropped the world's first atom bomb on the city of Hiroshima. Three days later, a plutonium bomb was dropped on Nagasaki. Around 160,000 Japanese civilians died in the two raids. The Soviet Union joined the Allies in the war against Japan, and the Japanese finally surrendered on August 15, 1945.

The End of the Old Order
TIME CHART

	EUROPE/USA	RUSSIA/CHINA/FAR EAST	MIDDLE EAST	REST OF THE WORLD
AD				
1901	Death of Queen Victoria			
1902				End of the Boer War in South Africa
1904>1905		Russo-Japanese war		
1905		General strike in Russia, riots in St. Petersburg		
1908			Young Turks revolt overthrows Turkey's traditional leadership	
1914>1918	World War I begins with the shooting of a little-known Austrian archduke, Francis Ferdinand, in Serbia			
1915			Turkey enters World War I on Germany's side	
1916	Easter Rising in Dublin – Irish challenge Britain's rule			Belgian forces occupy parts of German East Africa
1917		Russian revolution – Bolsheviks overthrow provisional government	Balfour Declaration – Britain favors the setting up of a Jewish state in Palestine	
1918>1920		Civil war in Russia		
1919	Treaty of Versailles – US, France and Britain demand reparation terms from a defeated Germany. League of Nations established		France is given a mandate by the League of Nations to govern Syria and Lebanon	Britain is given German East Africa which is then renamed Tanganyka (now Tanzania) In India, demonstrators are massacred at Amritsar.
1922	Mussolini becomes dictator of Italy			Indian civil rights leader Gandhi is imprisoned
1928				Indian National Congress demands independence from Britain
1929	Wall Street Crash precipitates world recession	China – Mao Zedong sets up Red Army	Arab-Jewish rioting in Palestine	
1933	Hitler becomes chancellor of Germany			
1934	Roosevelt's "New Deal" legislation introduces social and economic reforms in the USA	Non-aggression pact between Stalin and Hitler		
1935				Italy invades Ethiopia
1936>1939	Spanish Civil War			
1937>1945		Japan invades and occupies parts of China		
1939>1945	World War II – Germany invades Poland. Britain and France declare war on Germany			
1941		Hitler launches Operation Barbarossa, the invasion of Russia Japan declares war		
1943	Allied invasion of Italy		Italy invades Egypt from its colony in Libya	
1944	Allied invasion of Normandy			
1945	Germany is defeated on May 8, VE Day	US drops atom bombs on Hiroshima and Nagasaki. Japan surrenders		

Nuclear states

States with access
to nuclear weapons

States able to assemble
nuclear weapons

States wanting
nuclear weapons

PART TWO

Creating a New World

The balance of world power changed dramatically after World War II. The United States of America and the Soviet Union emerged as superpowers and their influence was felt in every country of the world. The rivalry between the two superpowers was illustrated by the space race, in which the US and USSR developed spacecraft and rockets that were capable of launching satellites.

Through its Marshall aid program, which it developed in order to stop communism from spreading, the US helped European countries to rebuild their bombed-out factories and re-establish their industries. The countries of western Europe joined in a military alliance with the US against the Soviet Union. This was known as the North Atlantic Treaty Organization, NATO.

In eastern Europe, behind an "iron curtain," the Soviet Union forced its political ideas of communism on nations such as the Baltic states, Poland, Hungary, Czechoslovakia and Romania, which had previously been independent. However, in the late 1980s the power of the Soviet Union began to fade and many states were able to break away and form their own independent, democratic governments.

Outside Europe, the Middle East has been in an almost constant state of conflict. The Palestinians have been trying to recover their homeland, which became a part of the new Israeli state in 1947. The increasing strength of the Islamic religion has also brought many oil-producing Arab states into conflict with the countries of the West.

The decline of colonial powers led to former colonies, mainly in Africa and Asia, gaining their independence. In spite of being free from colonial control, most are still economically dependent on countries of the developed world and are facing huge problems in feeding and educating their people.

The challenge now facing all the peoples of the world is to find a way in which the human race can live in balance with the Earth's resources.

The Post-War Settlement

THE DIVISION OF EUROPE

Left. Trailing their few possessions in broken carts, millions of refugees trudged across Europe in search of permanent homes.

Below. The three most powerful Allied leaders, Churchill, Roosevelt and Stalin, met at Yalta after the war to discuss the division of Europe after the defeat of Germany. They decided to give part of Poland to Russia and part of east Germany became part of Poland.

A t the end of World War II, people all over the world had to rebuild their lives.

THE RESISTERS During the war, groups of people – known as resistance movements – in countries that had been taken over by the Germans, worked against the soldiers occupying their countries. For example, they bombed trains carrying supplies to the German army. Towards the end of the war, these groups helped the Allies to free their countries from Nazi rule. Communist groups formed the core of many resistance movements. When the war ended, resistance groups temporarily governed their newly liberated countries and helped to restore civilian governments.

Resistance movements gave rough justice to people who had supported the Nazis. In France, for example, it is thought that around 5,000 of these people were executed without trial.

Meanwhile, those leaders of Nazi Germany who had been captured were put on trial at Nuremburg in Germany. Altogether, 12 Nazis were sentenced to death and seven were given long prison sentences.

REFUGEES At the end of the war, there were millions of *refugees* in Europe trying to find their way home. Some of them were people who had been taken from their homes

by the Germans and sent to other countries to act as slave labor, for example in factories in Germany itself. Others were Jews and political prisoners who had spent the war in *concentration camps* and were lucky to have survived. Some people had lost their homes in the fighting, or were now moving westwards because they were afraid of coming under the control of the Red Army in eastern Europe.

The Allies had to identify and care for these people, and somehow return them to their homes. This was a difficult task, as many had no papers to show where they came from.

Among all these innocent refugees there were also

Above. Christian Dior's 'New Look': post-war women's fashions went for soft, sweeping lines when clothing eventually came off ration.

Above. The fall of Berlin, April 30, 1945, liberated by the Soviets. A Russian soldier plants the red flag on top of the chancellory building, the Reichstag, in the center of the city. Berlin suffered horribly in the final days of the war and much of it was completely destroyed.

1 In 1949 the Communists won control of the Hungarian parliament. The new Soviet-style constitution was unpopular and in 1956 riots broke out in the capital, Budapest. Some concessions were made but then Soviet troops moved in to crush the uprising and many more Communist reforms followed. In 1989 Hungary returned to democratic rule.

2 In 1945 the partisan leader Tito became prime minister of a Communist Yugoslavia. After 1953 he became president and managed to keep good relations with the West and the USSR and the country relatively prosperous. In 1991 the union of states within Yugoslavia began to fall apart with fighting between Serbs and Croats.

Rudolf Hess

Rudolf Hess was one of the most important members of the German Nazi Party at the beginning of the war. In 1941, on the eve of the German invasion of Russia, Hess flew to Scotland to try and persuade the British to make peace with Germany. He was immediately arrested and imprisoned in the Tower of London. At the end of the war a series of trials were held to punish those who had been involved in war crimes. Hess was tried for his part in running the Nazi regime. He was found guilty and imprisoned for life.

some Nazis trying to escape from justice. Because of the confused situation, it was easy for some of these men to "disappear," and to reappear months or years later in a different town or country, using different names. Many escaped to places such as South America, where they made new lives for themselves.

EAST AND WEST At the end of the war, Soviet troops occupied half of Germany and almost all of eastern Europe. At a conference between the Allies in 1945, US President Franklin Roosevelt had promised Stalin a "*sphere of influence*" in the countries that the USSR had occupied.

The Soviets took over Latvia, Lithuania and Estonia in northwest Europe. They also encouraged the setting up of Communist governments in countries on the USSR's eastern border – Poland, Hungary, Romania and Czechoslovakia. They drew new boundaries for Poland, absorbing the eastern parts of that country into the Soviet Union and adding a large part of what was once Germany to the west.

The eastern part of Germany, which had been occupied by Soviet troops, became the Communist state of East Germany. Within East Germany, however, the city of Berlin remained under the joint control of the Allies: Britain, France, the US and the USSR.

THE COLD WAR

The "Cold War" is the name given to the period following World War II when relations between the Soviet Union and the United States of America became very bad and even hostile. After the war, the countries of East and West formed themselves into two opposing groups. In the West was the North Atlantic Treaty Organization (NATO), made up of the United States of America and its European allies, including Britain and France. In the East, the USSR and the Communist states around it formed an alliance called the Warsaw Pact.

THE SPREAD OF COMMUNISM Communist groups in Europe that had helped organize resistance to the Nazis during the war (see page 42) attracted popular support. In countries such as France and Italy, many Communists were elected as politicians and trade union organizers. The United States of America tried to prevent the spread of communism in Europe by giving financial aid to countries that had been ruined by the war. This program, called the Marshall Plan, was launched in June 1947.

The Cold War 1945–1989

Above. In 1955 the eight eastern European Communist governments came together to sign the Warsaw Pact. Under the agreement the armies of these states were placed under one command. **A large part of the Warsaw Pact army was stationed in East Germany to act as a threat to western Europe. These countries lay behind what Churchill called the "iron curtain."**

- North Atlantic Treaty Organisation NATO
- Warsaw Pact
- Neutral countries

The Berlin Wall

In June 1948, trouble broke out when the USSR tried to blockade the Allied-controlled sectors of Berlin to force the British and American occupying forces to leave. Berlin was cut off from West Germany but Allied aircraft flew in food and essential supplies.

The Berlin airlift lasted until May 1949

when the Soviets re-opened the borders. However, in 1961 the Soviets built a high fortified wall around their sector of the city. Many East Berliners were shot trying to escape over the wall to the freedom of the West. The notorious Berlin Wall was finally removed in 1989.

Above. Soviet tanks set up a road block in the city of Prague. When Czechoslovakia threatened to leave the Soviet Union in 1968, the Red Army was sent to restore Soviet rule and to depose the Czech president, Alexander Dubcek, who had tried to break away from Soviet control.

THE IRON CURTAIN In 1948 Russia encouraged a revolution in Czechoslovakia which brought in a Communist government. Every country in eastern Europe now had a Communist government, all controlled from Moscow. The Soviets tried to stop people in these countries from going to western Europe. The British prime minister, Winston Churchill, compared this to "*an iron curtain*" coming down across Europe.

The US and its European allies were determined to halt the spread of communism in Europe and around the world. The Cold War started in 1948, when the Soviets besieged the western part of Berlin, which was controlled by Britain, France and the US. The West responded by bringing in supplies.

The first open conflict between Communist and western forces was the Korean War, which began in 1950. The Communist army of North Korea, supported by the USSR and China, invaded South Korea. The US sent troops to support the South Koreans. The North Koreans were defeated in 1953.

THE ARMS RACE In 1949 the Soviets successfully tested a nuclear bomb. This was the start of a race between the USSR and US to see who could build the most nuclear weapons.

Technology developed for space travel became part of the arms race. In 1957, the USSR launched the satellite *Sputnik I* into orbit around the Earth. It was now possible to build a rocket with a nuclear warhead that could hit a target accurately from a long distance. The

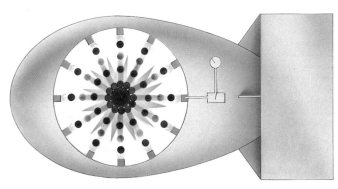

An atomic bomb, like the ones dropped on Hiroshima and Nagasaki in 1945. Both the US and the USSR made enough weapons to destroy the Earth many times over.

Americans and the Soviets stationed missiles in Europe that were aimed at each other. The ever-increasing number of missiles made the risk of a third world war seem more likely.

TREATIES The Nuclear Test-Ban Treaty of 1963 was the first step in a gradual process of talks between the USSR and the US about the development of nuclear weapons. Both sides began to reduce their numbers of these weapons after the first Strategic Arms Limitation Talks Treaty, SALT I, in 1972.

In spite of regular talks, the Cold War continued to exist between the two world powers for many years. However, after Mikhail Gorbachev became leader of the USSR in 1985, these attitudes began to change. Partly because they believed Gorbachev was making efforts to improve life in the Soviet Union for his people, the US trusted him more. The Cold War came to an end.

Korean War 1950–1953

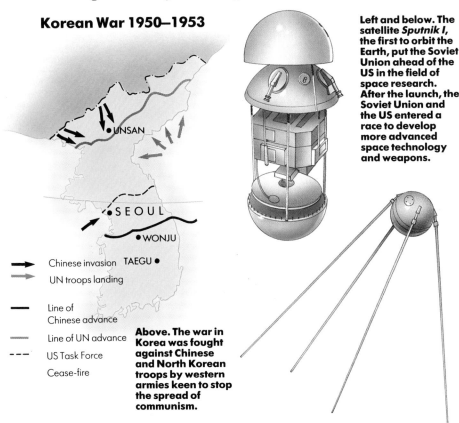

Chinese invasion

UN troops landing

Line of
Chinese advance

Line of UN advance

US Task Force

Cease-fire

Above. The war in Korea was fought against Chinese and North Korean troops by western armies keen to stop the spread of communism.

Left and below. The satellite *Sputnik I*, the first to orbit the Earth, put the Soviet Union ahead of the US in the field of space research. After the launch, the Soviet Union and the US entered a race to develop more advanced space technology and weapons.

Gorbachev

In 1985, Mikhail Gorbachev was elected leader of the Soviet Union. He wanted to change the Soviet political system through *perestroika*, restructuring, and *glasnost*, openness. Following electoral reforms, East European peoples held democratic elections in 1989 and got rid of their Communist leaders, and East and West Germany were reunited.

Gorbachev has achieved reductions in nuclear and conventional weapons through talks with President Reagan, left. He pledged a return to a capitalist system, but lost power in 1992.

THE DECLINE OF EMPIRES

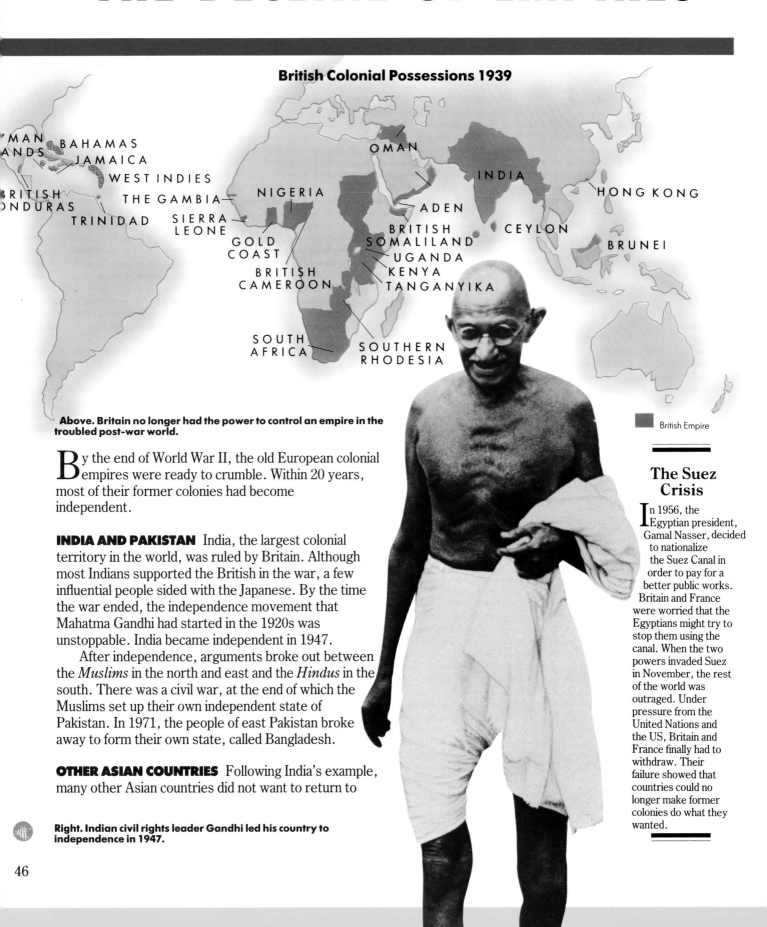

British Colonial Possessions 1939

MAN
ANDS
BAHAMAS
JAMAICA
WEST INDIES
BRITISH
ONDURAS
THE GAMBIA
TRINIDAD
SIERRA
LEONE
NIGERIA
GOLD
COAST
BRITISH
CAMEROON
SOUTH
AFRICA
OMAN
ADEN
BRITISH
SOMALILAND
UGANDA
KENYA
TANGANYIKA
SOUTHERN
RHODESIA
INDIA
CEYLON
HONG KONG
BRUNEI

British Empire

Above. Britain no longer had the power to control an empire in the troubled post-war world.

By the end of World War II, the old European colonial empires were ready to crumble. Within 20 years, most of their former colonies had become independent.

INDIA AND PAKISTAN India, the largest colonial territory in the world, was ruled by Britain. Although most Indians supported the British in the war, a few influential people sided with the Japanese. By the time the war ended, the independence movement that Mahatma Gandhi had started in the 1920s was unstoppable. India became independent in 1947.

After independence, arguments broke out between the *Muslims* in the north and east and the *Hindus* in the south. There was a civil war, at the end of which the Muslims set up their own independent state of Pakistan. In 1971, the people of east Pakistan broke away to form their own state, called Bangladesh.

OTHER ASIAN COUNTRIES Following India's example, many other Asian countries did not want to return to

Right. Indian civil rights leader Gandhi led his country to independence in 1947.

The Suez Crisis

In 1956, the Egyptian president, Gamal Nasser, decided to nationalize the Suez Canal in order to pay for a better public works. Britain and France were worried that the Egyptians might try to stop them using the canal. When the two powers invaded Suez in November, the rest of the world was outraged. Under pressure from the United Nations and the US, Britain and France finally had to withdraw. Their failure showed that countries could no longer make former colonies do what they wanted.

The Mau Mau

From 1952 until 1956, the Mau Mau, a group dedicated to removing the British, movement directed terrorist attacks against white settlers in the British colony of Kenya. Many settlers and their families were killed and their farms were set ablaze. Britain sent troops to track down the killers and the Mau Mau leader, Jomo Kenyatta, was imprisoned. In 1961, Kenyatta was released from prison. Three years later, he became Kenya's first president after winning democratic elections. Meanwhile the British colonies in Africa were gaining their independence. Ghana was the first, in 1957, followed by Nigeria (1960), Tanganyika and Sierra Leone (1961), Uganda (1962) and The Gambia (1963).

Above. Robert Mugabe was elected the first president of Zimbabwe, formerly the British colony of Rhodesia, in 1980.

Left. The French president General de Gaulle granted independence to the former French colonies Morocco and Tunisia in 1956. Britain set the pace for decolonization before World War II by granting independence to Canada, Australia, New Zealand and South Africa, then to India and Pakistan in 1947. Gradually the empires began to change to allow peoples the freedom to govern themselves.

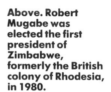

western rule in 1945. A rebellion in Indonesia led to independence from the Netherlands in 1949. In Indo-China, the Communists rebelled against their French rulers. The French, supported by the US, fought back but were defeated at the Battle of Dien Bien Phu in 1953 and were forced to leave. Indo-China was broken up to form Cambodia (Kampuchea), Laos and Vietnam.

Malaysia became independent from Britain in 1957. Now the only British colony in Asia is Hong Kong, which is due to be returned to Chinese rule in 1997.

AFRICA After World War II, the Allies freed Italy's former African colonies, Ethiopia and Libya. France granted independence to Morocco and Tunisia after rebellions there. But the French settlers in Algeria, who made up 10 percent of the population there, were fiercely opposed to any move towards Arab independence. The result was a war between the settlers and the Algerians that lasted four years and cost many lives. The defeated white settlers finally had to leave the country.

In many African countries, white settlers not only governed the country but also controlled its economy, legal system and armed forces. When these countries became independent, they had to begin to rebuild all

these systems and that sometimes led to problems. For example, after independence, there were civil wars in the former Belgian Congo, now Zaïre, and Nigeria.

RHODESIA AND SOUTH AFRICA Algeria was not the only country where the white settlers wanted to remain in control. In 1965, for example, Rhodesia rejected Britain's plans for its independence and the white government remained in place. The Africans in Rhodesia were kept out of power. Finally, after talks with the British government and African politicians, Rhodesia was renamed Zimbabwe and a democracy was set up in 1980.

South Africa was once part of the British Empire. Its white government voted to leave the Commonwealth and become a republic in 1961, because it did not want to share its power with the black South Africans.

Other countries have tried to persuade the country's white politicians to introduce changes to the country. Many countries refuse to sell certain items, such as weapons, to the South African government until it agrees to allow black people to vote (see pages 60–61).

INTERNATIONAL UNITY

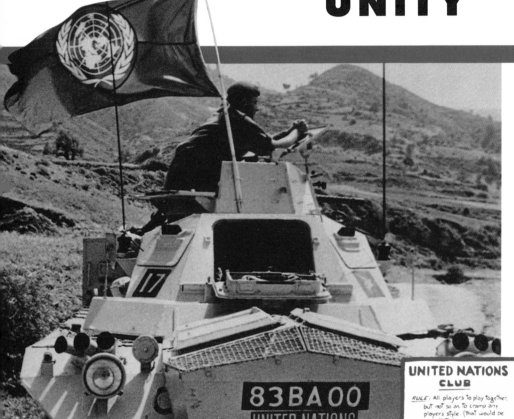

Above. A United Nations peacekeeping force keeps warring Greek and Turkish factions apart in Cyprus.

At the end of World War I, the League of Nations (see page 28) was set up to help solve problems between countries, but it was not successful. Since World War II, other international organizations have replaced it.

THE UNITED NATIONS The United Nations (UN) was founded in 1944. Representatives of countries meet to discuss international problems. Its aim is to reduce tension in the world and thus make war less likely.

The UN is headed by a secretary-general who is elected to lead the UN for five years. The General Assembly is made up of representatives from every country. If a majority of nations criticize the behavior of one member state, this can put pressure on that state to behave differently. In 1956, for example, the UN condemned France and Britain for invading Egypt over the Suez Canal (see page 46). This succeeded in preventing a war.

The UN Security Council has 11 members. Five of these – the USA, the USSR, Great Britain, France and China – are permanent members. The Council can vote

to take action against a member nation, or to send an armed force to keep the peace in an area where war is likely to break out. For example, UN troops were sent to Cyprus in 1965 to prevent a civil war between the Greek and Turkish communities.

But the UN has not always been successful. For instance, it has not prevented conflicts which have involved the interests of the US or the USSR. This is because any decision by the Security Council has to be unanimous, every member must agree with it. Each member has the right to veto, or say no to,

The former Allies failed to agree on common aims once Germany had been defeated.

any of the council's proposals. The US and the USSR have often used their vetoes to protect their own interests.

SETTING UP THE EEC After the damage done by World War II, the European countries needed to rebuild their bombed factories and start manufacturing goods for export. Some politicians called for western European countries to work together to re-establish trade links. This led to the Treaty of Rome in 1957, which set up the

The European Community

The United Nations

The United Nations has a number of specialized agencies which were set up to deal with major world problems.
The World Health Organization (WHO) aims to eradicate killer diseases such as malaria, smallpox and AIDS and improve the health of people all over the world through immunization and education programs.

The United Nations Educational, Scientific and Cultural Organization (UNESCO) is working to put an end to illiteracy and to ensure that people all over the world are given a basic education free.
The Food and Agriculture Organization (FAO) seeks to raise standards of nutrition by improving the quantity and quality of foods available around the world.

1 In 1979 the Soviet Union sent its troops into the Asian republic of Afghanistan. They set up a leader sympathetic to the Communists and claimed that they were invited guests of the new government. The Afghans waged a guerrilla war against the occupying forces and in 1989 the Soviet troops withdrew. They were beaten by American-funded groups of Islamic fighters called Mujahadeen, who then became locked in a civil war to find out who would run the country after the Russians had gone.

2 In 1982 the Argentine army invaded the Falkland Islands, which are British territory. The invasion was a result of a long dispute over who owned what the Argentinians called the *Malvinas*. The British government sent a task force to recapture the Islands. They landed on the Islands and after fierce fighting they defeated the poorly equipped Argentinian army, and re-took Port Stanley, the capital. This defeat led to the downfall of the military regime in Argentina and saw a return to democratic government.

The Red Cross

The International Red Cross is an organization dedicated to the relief of human suffering. Each country has an individual branch, but all work together to help others. The Red Cross was founded by a Swiss man called Jean Henri Dunant. He had witnessed the suffering of the wounded in the Austro-Sardinian war, and he wanted to find a way to help others in this situation. In 1863 a group of delegates met in Geneva to discuss the idea of an organization, and by 1864 the First Geneva

(Red Cross) Convention had been signed by 12 European nations. The convention laid down the way that prisoners of war should be treated and how the wounded should be helped. The symbol of the Red Cross, the red square on a white background is the reverse of the Swiss flag in honor of the founder.
Today the Red Cross works to help those injured in war.

European Economic Community (EEC). The treaty was signed by six countries – Belgium, the Netherlands, Luxembourg, France, Germany and Italy. Its main aim was to make it easier for these states to trade with each other. For instance, most countries put a tax on goods that are imported from other countries. The EEC wanted to abolish these taxes.

The six countries set up a European Parliament in Brussels, Belgium, to discuss matters that concerned all of them. They also set up a European Court in Strasbourg in France, to which people living in EEC countries could complain if they thought their country was treating them unfairly.

FROM THE SIX TO THE 12 In 1973 Britain, Ireland, Denmark and Portugal joined the EEC. Since then, Spain and Greece have also joined, bringing the number of members up to 12.

The EEC is now usually called the EC – the European Community – because it is no longer only interested in trade. It has become more involved in political issues relating to member states.

ISRAEL AND THE ARAB WORLD

American president Jimmy Carter, center, brings together Egyptian leader Anwar Sadat, left, and Israeli Premier Menachem Begin, right, for peace talks at Camp David.

The Jewish State of Israel has only been in existence since 1948, but for most of its short life it has been in conflict with its Arab neighbors. The reasons for the dispute can be traced back to the defeat of Turkey's Ottoman Empire in World War I, when the League of Nations put Britain temporarily in charge of Palestine.

THE BALFOUR DECLARATION In November 1917 the British government issued the Balfour Declaration: a promise to make Palestine a national home for the Jewish people who were scattered around the world.

Under British rule, Jewish *emigrants* began to settle in Palestine. These settlers often set up communities called *kibbutzim*, the Hebrew word for "groups," where everyone worked together.

By 1936 the stream of emigrants from Europe turned into a flood as Jews fled to escape *persecution* in Hitler's Germany (see page 30). This led to an uprising in Palestine. In order to keep the peace, Britain put a strict limit on the number of Jews coming to

Palestine. As a result, several ships carrying Jewish emigrants were turned away. One ship sank, killing all the people on board.

SETTING UP OF THE JEWISH STATE After the war, it was discovered that millions of Jews had been slaughtered in Nazi death camps. Britain and the rest of the western world felt the time had come to give the Jews a permanent home.

Britain handed Palestine over to the Jews, who proclaimed the new State of Israel in May 1948. Jews from all over the world came to settle in Israel and began to build the country, which developed rapidly.

WAR WITH THE ARABS Shortly after proclaiming its independence, Israel was attacked on all sides by five neighboring Arab states. By July, a well-organized Israeli army had defeated the Arabs. But Jordan captured Israeli land on the West Bank of the River Jordan, including the city of Jerusalem.

In June 1967, Israeli planes attacked the Arab forces that had been gathering on its borders. This was the start of the Six Day War. Within hours, Israel had destroyed the air forces and the airfields of Egypt, Syria and Jordan. Israeli land forces captured the whole of Jerusalem and the West Bank of the Jordan, and also took the Sinai Peninsula to the south.

INVOLVEMENT OF THE SUPER POWERS On October 5, 1973, the Jewish holy day of Yom Kippur, Arab armies – equipped and trained by the Soviet Union – launched a surprise attack on Israel. At first it seemed that they would overcome the unprepared Israeli army.

On the fifth day of the war, the US, which was Israel's ally, sent urgently needed equipment and modern fighter aircraft to help Israel's air force. The tide of war began to turn in Israel's favor.

In June 1967 the UN arranged a cease-fire and evacuated, Arab refugees.

Symbol of a divided city: the Golden Mosque in Jerusalem covers the rock from which Muhammed ascended into heaven.

Above. During the Six Day war in 1967, the Israeli scored major victories against the Arabs.

The Expansion of Israel 1947–1990

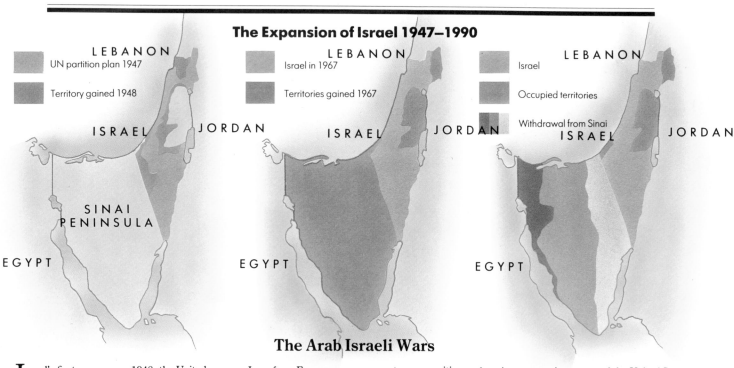

LEBANON
UN partition plan 1947
Territory gained 1948
ISRAEL
JORDAN
SINAI
PENINSULA
EGYPT

LEBANON
Israel in 1967
Territories gained 1967
ISRAEL
JORDAN
EGYPT

LEBANON
Israel
Occupied territories
Withdrawal from Sinai
ISRAEL
JORDAN
EGYPT

The Arab Israeli Wars

Israel's first elections brought David Ben Gurion, a former guerrilla leader, to power. Following the defeat of the Arab League nations in the war of 1948, the United Nations negotiated a series of truces. As a result of the threat to the fledgling state, Israel encouraged the immigration of massive numbers of Jews from Europe, eastern Europe, Russia and the United States. The influx of Jews tended to mean that Israel's native Palestinian people were pushed out into separate communities which were poor in terms of resources and land.

The rapidly growing population and the need to spend large amounts of money on keeping an army in a state of almost constant readiness caused Israel serious economic difficulties. But the country has had influential friends, particularly in Britain and the United States, and offers of military assistance were particularly helpful in the Yom Kippur War of 1970.

OIL AND ISLAM

The Middle East

OPEC

The Organization of Petroleum Exporting Countries was launched in 1960 to improve trading conditions for Third World petroleum-exporting states. It has 13 member states including Iran, Iraq, Kuwait, Libya, Qatar, Saudi Arabia and the United Arab Emirates. At the time, most oil wells in the Middle East were owned and operated by western companies. By the early 1970s most wells had been nationalized by their respective Arab governments.

During the 1973 war against Israel, the Arab states realized they could exert pressure by cutting off oil supplies to Israel's allies. Iran took the lead in raising prices, and between 1973 and 1974 the price of oil increased by 500 percent, leading to a deep recession in the West.

Since the late 1970s, Saudi Arabia, an ally of the US, has kept its oil production high and this has tended to stabilize the price of oil.

Iranians celebrate the return of Ayatollah Khomeini, their religious leader.

The area we know as the Middle East stretches from Libya in the west to Iran in the east. This area produces over half the oil and natural gas used in the western world. Oil has made some countries, like Saudi Arabia, Qatar and the United Arab Emirates, very rich indeed. However, other countries in the area are among the poorest in the world.

SUEZ Although the Arab countries had been dominated by colonial powers for many centuries, after World War II they began to show their independence. One of the first examples of this was the decision of Egypt's President Gamal Nasser to seize control of the Suez Canal in 1959. At that time the canal was owned and operated jointly by Britain and France. Nasser's action led to a force of British and French troops invading Suez. Pressure from the United States and the United Nations soon forced them to withdraw.

IRAN The most important religion of the Middle East is *Islam*. When the people of Iran rose up against their shah, the monarch, in 1979, Islamic holy men helped to organize the revolution. An Islamic republic was set up under Ayatollah Khomeini, a religious leader who had been outlawed by the shah and who had been forced to live in exile in France.

The new Islamic state introduced strict religious laws and cut off relations with the West. A group of students took over the US embassy in Tehran, the capital of Iran, and held its staff hostage to bargain for the release of Iranian property in the US, which had previously belonged to the shah's government.

War also broke out with Iraq over territory around the oil port of Basra, which both countries claimed. Religious differences in the war soon developed, as Iraq's government did not follow the *fundamentalist* form of religion that was practiced by Iran.

Western countries such as Britain, France and Germany sold arms openly to Iraq, while the US made secret arms deals with Iran in order to speed the return of the US embassy hostages. The hostages were finally released in 1981.

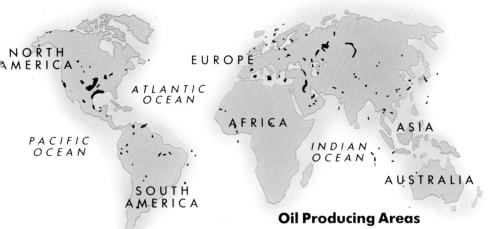

Oil Producing Areas

Above. This map shows the positions of the important oil fields around the world.

SOVIET UNION 4,464,000,000 barrels	
UNITED STATES 3,194,000,000 barrels	
SAUDI ARABIA 1,659,000,000 barrels	
MEXICO 1,001,000,000 barrels	
GREAT BRITAIN 895,000,000 barrels	
CHINA 821,000,000 barrels	
IRAN 791,000,000 barrels	
VENEZUELA 629,000,000 barrels	
CANADA 522,000,000 barrels	
NIGERIA 516,000,000 barrels	

In barrels of 42-gallon capacity; figures are for 1984
Source: Oil and GasJournal, Dec 31. 1984

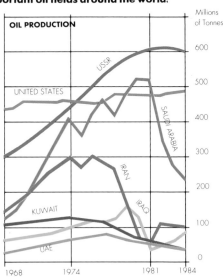

OIL PRODUCTION

Millions of Tonnes

USSR — UNITED STATES — SAUDI ARABIA — IRAN — IRAQ — KUWAIT — UAE

1968 1974 1981 1984

Left. A graph to show the output of some of the world's major oil-producing countries. The Soviet Union is still the world's largest producer.

Above. Some Middle Eastern oil producers have deliberately lowered their output to force other states to pay more for their oil.

The Gulf

The Gulf States include Saudi Arabia, Bahrain, Oman, Qatar, Kuwait and the United Arab Emirates (UAE).

In spite of being the richest Arab nations, they are also among the most backward-looking. The tiny states are governed by old-fashioned monarchies, there is little democracy, and members of the Arab royal families fulfil the functions of ministers of state.

Most Gulf States observe a very strict Islamic law with prohibition of alcohol and traditional penalties such as the use of corporal punishment to deal with some crimes.

The reason for the political stability is that a high standard of living is enjoyed by all Arab families; income per head is among the highest in the world. Their very high standard of living has enabled many wealthy families to enjoy luxury goods bought from the West and also to invest overseas.

However, the fact that the Arab populations of these states are so small means that they have to employ large numbers of overseas workers, particularly in their armed forces, domestic service and construction industries.

Saudi Arabia is by far the richest oil state with the biggest oil reserves and the highest oil production of any Arab nation. Saudi Arabia produces roughly three times as much oil as the other Gulf States put together and almost as much oil as the rest of the Arab oil-producing nations. Saudi Arabia exports most of its oil to the West and, more than any other nation, is responsible for setting a world price for oil by either increasing or decreasing its production.

Beirut, capital of Lebanon, is the focus for the civil war that has raged in the country since 1975.

THE GULF WAR The Iran-Iraq war ended in 1988, but in August 1990 the Iraqi leader, Saddam Hussein, invaded Kuwait. He claimed that Kuwait had originally belonged to Iraq before the western powers had established a monarchy there after the fall of the Ottoman Empire in 1918. The United Nations condemned this invasion and some western countries, led by the US and Britain, sent troops to the area. Some Arab countries, including Saudi Arabia and Syria, supported this action. When the Iraqis had not withdrawn from Kuwait by January 1991, the Allies attacked the Iraqi troops in Kuwait. Within a few weeks, the Allied forces had pushed Saddam Hussein's army back to the borders of Iraq.

LEBANON The conflict between Israel and its Arab neighbors (see pages 50–51) spilled over into Lebanon in 1975 after Israel attacked Palestinian bases in Lebanon. Civil war broke out. Even after the Palestinians withdrew from the capital city of Beirut, fighting continued between Christian *Druze* forces and Shi-ite Moslems who were supplied with arms by Iran and Syria.

VIETNAM

The Vietnam War 1965—1973

Although Americans placed over half a million troops in South Vietnam and launched huge bombing raids against the North, they failed to win against the local guerrilla army. The US pulled out its troops in 1973.

→ Ho Chi Minh Trail

Under communist control

Under government control

Contested areas

NORTH VIETNAM

HANOI

LAOS

THAILAND

BANGKOK

CAMBODIA

PHNOM PENH

SOUTH VIETNAM

SAIGON

In February 1965, at the height of the Cold War (see pages 44–45), American troops arrived in South Vietnam to fight the spread of communism in Asia. The South Vietnamese government was under attack from North Vietnam and from Communist insurgents – the Viet Cong – within its own country.

AN UNWINNABLE WAR Americans tried without success to fight a traditional war against the Viet Cong. But the Viet Cong moved about constantly and avoided open battles. By day, they hid their weapons and looked like ordinary peasants; by night they launched small-scale raids. On many occasions, American forces killed innocent Vietnamese peasants, mistaking them for their enemy.

But killing innocent civilians only made the Americans more unpopular in Vietnam and helped the Viet Cong to win more support. When the US forces stepped up the action against North Vietnam by bombing stores of weapons and supplies, the Viet Cong became more determined to fight back. In any case, no amount of American bombing could ever cut off the supply of arms to the rebels, as the Soviet Union and China were supplying weapons and aid to North Vietnam. All around the world, people became more and more opposed to the American involvement in Vietnam as the war dragged on. This opposition increased when the Americans bombed Vietnamese villages with a substance called *napalm*, which set fire to the villages.

Bring Our Boys Home

American public opinion could no longer tolerate the high casualty rate among the troops and the seemingly senseless destruction of North Vietnam and Cambodia by mass bombing raids. A very strong anti-war movement gathered force within the US. President Johnson did not stand for re-election. His successor, Richard Nixon, reduced the number of American troops and increased aid to help the South Vietnamese strengthen their own army.

Left. South Vietnamese children run in terror from their burning village, destroyed by fighting between the US troops and the Viet Cong guerrillas.

Above. North Vietnamese leader Ho Chi Minh founded the Vietnamese Communist Party in 1930. He led North Vietnam until his death in 1969.

THE TET OFFENSIVE On January 31, 1968, the Viet Cong and the North Vietnamese launched a major attack, called the Tet Offensive, against the US and South Vietnamese forces. Although the Viet Cong attack was defeated, the fact that they could launch an attack at all after all the bombing raids that had been carried out against them, made politicians in America realize that they could not win the war.

During the early 1970s, the US increased its bombing raids on North Vietnam and on neighboring Cambodia, which it thought was supplying arms to the Viet Cong. The United States hoped to force the North Vietnamese to begin peace talks.

THE US WITHDRAWAL In 1973, the United States of America and the North Vietnamese finally signed a cease-fire. The US began to withdraw most of its forces, leaving South Vietnam to defend itself. But peace between the North and the South was only temporary. By the beginning of 1975, North Vietnamese forces had begun to advance on the South. In April, President Thieu of South Vietnam escaped to Taiwan. Within days, the last American soldiers left Vietnam and the longest war in the USA's history came to an end. A few hours later, North Vietnamese troops captured the South Vietnamese capital city of Saigon and took over the country.

A Vietnamese village. The Americans found fighting against the North Vietnamese difficult as conventional methods of warfare failed. The Viet Cong soldiers lived as normal peasants in the villages and came out at night in small groups to attack the enemy.

RED CHINA

The "Great Leap Forward" organized people into self-sufficient groups, producing everything they needed to eat and all their clothes and household and farming equipment.

The history of China after the Second World War is the history of the Chinese Communist Party. It is a history shaped by just one man – Mao Zedong.

After the Japanese had been driven from China at the end of World War II, Mao's Red Army fought to take control of the vast country from Chiang Kai-shek Chinese Nationalist Party. The Communists finally captured the capital, Beijing, in January 1949. Mao proclaimed the People's Republic of China in October.

REFORMS Like Russia in the nineteenth century, China was a vast country containing many different ethnic groups. Most of the population were peasants, who lived in villages in conditions of great poverty. One of Mao Zedong's first acts on becoming chairman, leader, of the new People's Republic was to take large farms away from wealthy private landlords and divide the land up among the poor. The landlords were treated harshly. Most were executed; it is believed that during the early years of the new republic between one and two million landlords were killed.

However, the change in land ownership was not enough to feed China's rapidly growing population, which

The Long March 1948

Above. Mao Zedong led his Communists on the "Long March" to escape enemies and set up a new power base.

▨	Area of Nationalist authority
▨	Area of Communist authority
- - -	Route of Long March

In 1934, Mao Zedong tried to lead a Communist uprising with a large force of peasant volunteers – the Red Army. When Chinese government troops surrounded his base, Mao decided the only way to keep Chinese communism alive was to retreat towards the northern mountains.

Thus began the famous Long March. Mao led an army of 90,000 people for 6,000 miles over 368 days. At the end of the Long March, Mao was elected Chairman of the Chinese Communist Party.

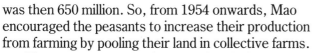

Left. A Communist poster shows members of the armed forces and workers cheering their leader, Mao Zedong.

Right. Deng Xiaoping was leader of the Chinese Communist Party during the pro-democracy student uprisings in 1989.

Above. Hong Kong, on the coast of southern China, is one of the world's most important financial and trading centers. After a war with China, Britain was granted the right to govern Hong Kong for 99 years. This lease expires in 1997 when Britain will have to return the colony to China.

was then 650 million. So, from 1954 onwards, Mao encouraged the peasants to increase their production from farming by pooling their land in collective farms.

The government also invested in building roads and railways and in power generation projects. Because of high taxes, industrialists often preferred to hand over their businesses to the government, which then employed them as managers.

CHINESE ISOLATION During the 1950s, the Soviet Union helped China to develop its economy by giving it large amounts of financial aid and by sending scientists and technicians to help the Chinese set up modern factories. From 1960, relations between the two Communist countries became strained as China turned inwards and became concerned only with rebuilding its society.

The Chinese government introduced two important changes to the country. The "Great Leap Forward" in 1958 reorganized people into living in groups that were self-sufficient, producing all their own food and goods. Both agricultural and industrial output fell dramatically and so too did China's exports to the rest of the world.

The "Cultural Revolution" of 1966 forced all artists and intellectuals to work on the land. This resulted in an enormous waste of talent and a decline in standards of education. During this period, many books were burned and people were encouraged to read *The Little Red Book of Collected Thoughts of Chairman Mao*.

PRESENT-DAY CHINA When Chairman Mao died in 1976, two rival groups fought for control of the country. On one side, Deng Xiaoping wanted limited reforms and some development of western ideas. On the other side was the "Gang of Four," including Mao's widow, who wanted to continue the strict policies of the Cultural Revolution.

Deng Xiaoping became head of state in 1977 and began to open up trade with the West. He also introduced a strict policy of one child per family in an attempt to stop the country's huge population from growing any further. However, the Chinese government has dealt harshly with many of its people who have called for the country to become a democracy. China has also dealt harshly with the independence movement in Tibet.

Beliefs and the Fight for Ideas

RELIGION

Religion gives people moral rules by which to live their lives, but when it is taken to extremes it can make some people very intolerant of other people's beliefs.

EASTERN EUROPE When the Communists took power in Russia in 1917 (see pages 24–25), they wanted to put an end to religious beliefs, which they thought were nothing more than *superstitions* that would divide people's loyalty to the state.

Governments in eastern Europe after the Second World War disapproved of all religions. In some countries, such as the Soviet Union, it was against the law to practice religion. Believers could be sent to prison or to a psychiatric hospital if they were caught worshipping together. Jews were treated especially badly. They were not allowed to worship, and for many years they were also refused permission to emigrate to Israel.

When Communist control of eastern Europe crumbled at the end of the 1980s, so too did the ban on religious activities. Romanian revolutionaries celebrated the fall of their Communist dictator, Nikolai Ceaucescu, with church services held in the open air. In 1989, *Russian Orthodox* Christians celebrated Christmas openly in Moscow for the first time since the Revolution.

THE MIDDLE EAST The foundation of the Jewish state in Israel and the involvement of the United States of America in the politics of the Middle East has sparked off a revival of the traditional Arab religion of Islam.

Most Arab states are hostile towards Israel, mainly because of their support for the Palestinian Arab population which lived in the area before Israel was founded. Civil war broke out in Lebanon when Palestinian refugees from Israel settled there and upset the delicate balance between the country's Christian and Muslim

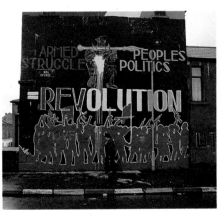

Above. After years of suppression under Communist rule, a Russian Orthodox priest holds an Easter service in St. Valentine's Cathedral, Kiev, Ukraine.

Right. Religion can lead to conflict. This graffiti in Belfast, Northern Ireland, is a symbol of revolt by the IRA against British rule in the province.

NORTH AMERICA

SOUTH AMERICA

Christianity

Islam

Confucianism

Hinduism

Buddhism

Shintoism

Judaism

Natural and/or other

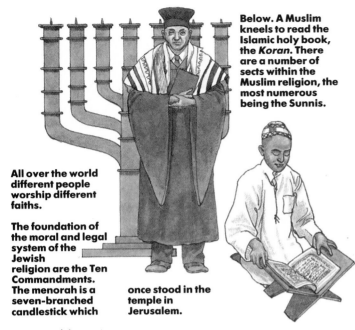

Below. A Muslim kneels to read the Islamic holy book, the *Koran*. There are a number of sects within the Muslim religion, the most numerous being the Sunnis.

All over the world different people worship different faiths.

The foundation of the moral and legal system of the Jewish religion are the Ten Commandments. The menorah is a seven-branched candlestick which once stood in the temple in Jerusalem.

communities.

There have also been wars between Islamic groups and nations. Iran and Iraq were at war for most of the 1980s, even though they were both Muslim countries. In the Gulf War of 1991 (see page 52), President Saddam Hussein of Iraq attacked both the Islamic kingdom of Kuwait and the Jewish state of Israel.

NORTHERN IRELAND When southern Ireland became independent in 1921, the northern province of Ulster stayed within the United Kingdom. Unlike the rest of Ireland, Ulster had a large Protestant community, whose ancestors were British. Its Catholic population was in the minority. Catholics who tried to get good jobs or houses were treated less favorably than Protestants and the community was sharply divided into two distinct religious groups. The Catholics began to protest about this.

Rioting broke out between the Protestant and Catholic communities in 1969 and the British army was sent to restore order. The army has been in Northern Ireland ever since.

By January 1970 the Provisional IRA (Irish Republican Army) had been formed to fight against the British army. It also attacked members of the Protestant community. Protestants formed a similar organization, called the Ulster Defence Association or UDA. The IRA wants Northern Ireland to be united to the Irish republic in the south, while the UDA wants it to remain part of the United Kingdom.

Since the unrest started, hundreds of soldiers, police and civilians have been killed, as well as many terrorists. Mistrust and hatred between the two religious communities continues, and the solutions as distant as ever.

World Religions

The many different religions of the world. The religion with the most followers is Christianity. The followers of Christianity are spread all over the world, but concentrated in the western hemisphere. Followers of Islam are found mainly in the Middle East and North Africa. The areas covered by particular religions generally follow the routes of trade or conquest of the people of that particular faith. Islam has moved from the Middle East towards western Europe, as did Christianity, which has spread from what is now Israel to the rest of the world.

EUROPE

CHINA

JAPAN

INDIA

AFRICA

AUSTRALIA

59

THE STRUGGLE FOR HUMAN RIGHTS

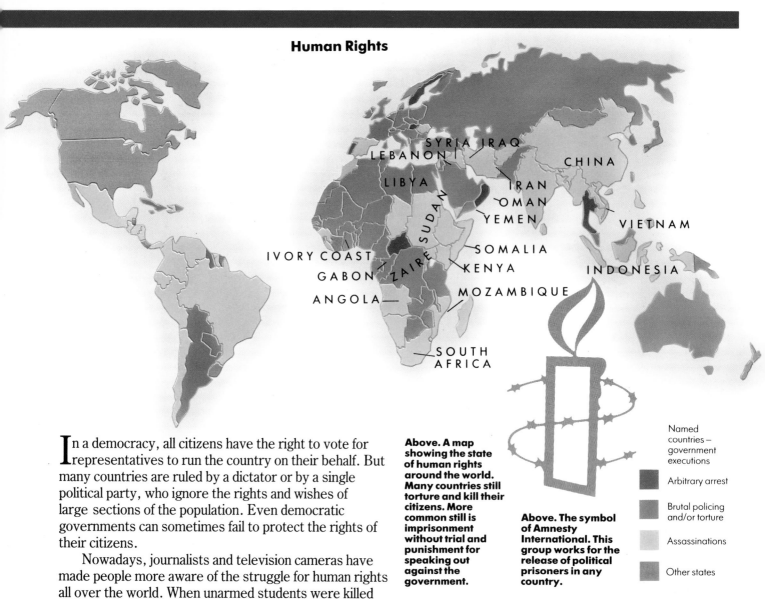

Human Rights

SYRIA IRAQ
LEBANON
LIBYA
CHINA
IRAN
OMAN
SUDAN
YEMEN
VIETNAM
IVORY COAST
SOMALIA
GABON ZAIRE
KENYA
INDONESIA
ANGOLA
MOZAMBIQUE
SOUTH
AFRICA

Above. A map showing the state of human rights around the world. Many countries still torture and kill their citizens. More common still is imprisonment without trial and punishment for speaking out against the government.

Above. The symbol of Amnesty International. This group works for the release of political prisoners in any country.

Named countries — government executions

Arbitrary arrest

Brutal policing and/or torture

Assassinations

Other states

In a democracy, all citizens have the right to vote for representatives to run the country on their behalf. But many countries are ruled by a dictator or by a single political party, who ignore the rights and wishes of large sections of the population. Even democratic governments can sometimes fail to protect the rights of their citizens.

Nowadays, journalists and television cameras have made people more aware of the struggle for human rights all over the world. When unarmed students were killed by troops in Tianenmen Square in Beijing, China, in June 1989, the world's attention was focused on the Chinese people's demand for a more democratic form of government.

HUMAN RIGHTS The Universal Declaration of Human Rights, issued by the United Nations in 1948, says that everyone should be treated "without distinction of any kind such as race, color, sex, language, religion, political or other opinion." But these human rights are not always upheld. According to the campaigning organization, Amnesty International, torture is still practiced in one-third of the countries in the world.

RACE Racial discrimination is the term for one *ethnic* group treating another group unfavorably simply because that group is different. Sadly, this behavior can be found in almost any part of the world.

During the 1960s, black people in the southern states of the US campaigned for the right to have the same education and job opportunities as white people. One of the leaders of this campaign was Dr. Martin Luther King, Jr. He was assassinated in 1968, but his "Freedom Riders" campaign was successful.

In South Africa, government has remained in the hands of a white minority. After 1961, when white South Africans voted to leave the British Commonwealth and

Above. In 1989, Chinese students filled Tiananmen Square in Beijing. They protested against the government and demanded democracy. Many were killed as the protest was brutally broken up.

Right. For many years, blacks in South Africa were banned from white areas.

STRAND EN SEE
NET BLANKES
BEACH AND SEA
WHITES ONLY

Above. Martin Luther King fought for equal rights for black people. He was shot dead in Memphis, Tennessee, in 1968.

Andrei Sakharov

Andrei Sakharov (1921–) won the Nobel Peace Prize in 1975 for his efforts in promoting human rights in what was the Soviet Union. He first became well known as a physicist. His work on controlled thermonuclear reactions helped the Soviet Union to develop the hydrogen bomb in the 1950s. He was exiled from Moscow in 1980 for speaking out against the government. Now he is an elected member of the Congress of People's Deputies.

become a republic (see page 47), the black population was treated completely differently from the white population. This policy, called *apartheid* or "apartness" in Afrikaans, meant, for example, that black and white people could not live in the same areas. The white government passed very tough laws to control its black population. They banned public meetings. Anyone who was suspected of being involved in anti-government activities was arrested and held without trial for 90 days.

Some of these rules were changed in the late 1980s, but black people in South Africa are still treated differently from the white population.

Nelson Mandela

Opposition to apartheid centred on an organization called the African National Congress or ANC. Nelson Mandela, one of the ANC leaders, was imprisoned from 1962 to 1989. His release was a sign that the Government was ready reform.

POLITICAL OPPOSITION Originally, the Russian Revolution had aimed to make people more free by ending the power of the tsars. But Joseph Stalin, the leader from 1924 to 1953, returned the country to a state of terror. His secret police arrested huge numbers of innocent Russian citizens who were suspected of plotting against him, and either executed them without trial or sent them to labor camps in Siberia, where many died. Several million people disappeared in this way.

Later Soviet leaders did not follow Stalin's extreme example, but they did use harsh treatment against anyone who criticized the Soviet system. People could not discuss ideas freely. Many books were banned and many writers were *exiled* to remote parts of the Soviet Union.

Mikhail Gorbachev (see page 45) began a policy of openness or *glasnost* when he became the Soviet leader in 1982. For the first time Russian newspapers were allowed to criticize the Communist system and writers were allowed to return from exile.

NEW IDEAS IN THE ARTS

Elvis Presley performs "Jailhouse Rock." He brought a new excitement to rock and roll.

Since World War II, the culture and life-style of the United States of America has had an enormous influence on the rest of the developed world. The US was by far the wealthiest country after the war. It was also the first to develop a *consumer society*, where more people had more money and looked for more things on which to spend that money.

By the early 1960s, most European countries had overcome the economic problems of the post-war years. Many people, particularly the young, found that they had greater incomes and increased leisure time.

THE ROCK AND ROLL YEARS After the war, classical music built upon the changes that had occurred during the early years of the century. But more people were listening to a new type of music called rock and roll. American musicians such as Bill Haley, Chuck Berry, Fats Domino, Little Richard, Buddy Holly and Elvis Presley sang about rebelling against authority and became very popular with young people.

Films such as *Rebel Without a Cause*, starring James Dean, and *The Wild One*, starring Marlon Brando, were also about the problems and concerns of young people. The word "teenager" was used for the first time, and teenagers began to develop their own culture.

THE SWINGING SIXTIES In the 1960s, London became a center for pop culture and fashion. Groups like the Rolling Stones and the Beatles created their own unmistakable sound, while designers like Mary Quant and Barbara Hulaniki of Biba made Carnaby Street the fashion capital of the world. Clothes changed dramatically. Young women threw away girdles and stockings in favor of mini-skirts, tights and T-shirts.

Fashion was not the only thing that changed. People were more tolerant and broad-minded about what they saw and read. In many countries, *censorship* was relaxed. It was only after a court case in 1960 that people in Britain were allowed to read D. H. Lawrence's novel, *Lady Chatterley's Lover*. In 1968 two British theater productions, *Oh Calcutta!* and *Hair*, shocked the world when nude people appeared on stage. The second half of the century also produced some new novels which explored difficult themes such as the nature of violence and sexuality. Some of the most influential of these were William Golding's *Lord of the Flies*, J.D. Salinger's *Catcher in the Rye* and Hubert Selby's *Last Exit to Brooklyn*.

POP ART Youth culture created its own art, known as pop art. Its most famous artist was Andy Warhol. Pop art was almost anti-art; in fact, some people said it wasn't art at all.

Marlon Brando in the *Wild One*. This leather-clad look inspired generations of teenaged rebels.

Left. The Guggenheim Museum in New York. It exhibits modern art.

Frank Lloyd Wright

One of the most influential of all twentieth-century architects was Frank Lloyd Wright. Wright's career began in 1890 and spanned six decades.

Wright's imaginative designs were applied not just to large public buildings but to houses which he believed should fit in with the surrounding landscape. He made bold use of both traditional and new building materials like ferro-concrete and always claimed that his inspiration lay "in the nature of materials."

Wright's last major work and his most famous was the Guggenheim Museum in New York City.

1 Sport during the 1960s saw the development of the competitor as star. Cassius Clay, later Mohammed Ali, became heavyweight boxing champion of the world. At the Olympics in Mexico in 1968 black American athletes gave the "black power" salute when they collected their medals, to protest for equal rights.

2 Increasing affluence began to give people more time for leisure activity. The blockbuster film was very popular, with movies like *Ben Hur* costing millions but taking more. More people than ever before (in the West) owned televisions and cars.

Left. *Whaam!* by Roy Litchenstein. Pop art explored the images of a consumer society and modern mass-production. Other examples include Andy Warhol's pictures of a soup can and of screen idol Marilyn Monroe.

Right. London became the fashion capital of the swinging sixties. Mary Quant and other designers worked from Carnaby Street, which was filled with shops selling the new look.

Above. Jean-Paul Sartre, the French existentialist thinker and writer. His theory that we only become something through thought and deed was very influential.

Left. The student riots in Paris in 1968. There was rioting in many countries against the ruling parties.

Towards 2000

THE DEVELOPING WORLD

Left. Women wash their cooking pots in an open drain in the street in a village in Bangladesh.

Below. A flooded village in Africa. Such disasters in developing countries require immediate aid from richer nations both to solve the immediate problems of providing food, shelter and medical aid as well as trying to re-establish the stricken communities.

The developing world, also known as the Third World, consists of poor countries that have little manufacturing industry of their own, where the majority of the population are peasants who live in extreme poverty in the countryside.

GEOGRAPHY AND CLIMATE Most of these countries are situated in Africa, the Indian sub-continent, South America, the Middle East and the Far East. The hot climate in these areas, combined with too much or too little rainfall and poor soils, makes farming difficult.

Unfortunately, these areas also tend to suffer from natural disasters, such as earthquakes, high winds and flooding, which destroy life, property, farming land and livestock. In Bangladesh, for example, a tidal wave in 1991

Mother Teresa won the Nobel Peace Prize in 1979 for her work in looking after orphans in Calcutta.

flooded a vast area of low-lying agricultural land, killing at least 100,000 people. Most of the cattle were also drowned, and the survivors were left with no food and no way to rebuild their ruined farms.

SERVICES AND JOBS The governments of developing countries are not usually able to provide the services that people in the developed world take for granted, like well-made roads, transport, education, health care and sick pay. Employment is scarce and low-paid. Often, an employed person has to support a large number of *dependants*, such as children or elderly relatives.

Aid Programs

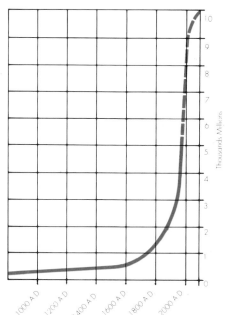

It is in the interests of the developed world to help Third World countries improve their own industries and reduce their dependence on single commodities. Many aid packages provide money for major civil engineering projects, such as building dams or power stations, that will improve a nation's economy. Over a number of years, aid will improve trade links and be of mutual benefit.

As well as receiving direct aid, many developing countries have borrowed from richer countries. High interest on loans has made many of them even poorer. If they could borrow money more cheaply, they would be better able to carry out aid programs.

Above. This graph shows how the human population has increased since AD 800. Until 1600 the number of people grew steadily. After this the numbers began to grow very rapidly. Today the world population is close to six billion. If the rate stays the same there will be ten billion people on the planet by the end of the 21st century, on a planet which cannot adequately feed half that number.

Poor Nations

Food available

■ Above average

■ Below average

The world is sharply divided into wealthy and poor nations.

CASH CROPS Many developing countries were once colonies whose economies were organized to suit the needs of their colonial rulers. As a result, they were never allowed to grow all their own food, or to develop manufacturing industries. Instead, the land was used to produce a limited number of food crops to send to the country that governed them.

This history can be seen today in countries that still concentrate on growing one type of crop, which is exported for cash to pay for imports such as industrial machinery. Examples of such *cash crops* are coffee from Kenya, tea from Tanzania, cotton from Sudan and cocoa from Ghana. Zaïre's economy depends on mining copper.

Under the cash crop system, less land is available for growing crops and raising livestock to feed the country's population. It is very risky for a country to depend too much on one crop. If a disease affects the crop, or there is a drought, the country has nothing to export. If too much of the crop is produced, this may lead to a sudden fall in the price on the world market.

POPULATION GROWTH AND POVERTY The chief problem faced by most developing countries is that their population is expanding faster than their income. Traditionally, many people have large families because many of their children die when they are babies, and they want to ensure that at least one child will survive to look after them in their old age. But improvements in medical care mean that more of these children are growing up to be adults, so the populations are soaring. Meanwhile, the money that is received from trade is not enough for the growing populations. These countries are still dependent on the West for aid, or cash help.

Poverty is made worse by the increasing problem of famine. If the government is weak, this can lead to a revolution. It seems unlikely that these countries will become settled and peaceful until their citizens have won a greater share of the world's prosperity and food.

Above. The ENIAC, Electronic Numerator Integrator and Calculator, was the first modern computer. It took up a whole room and was less powerful than a modern calculator.

Right. Robots can now perform the work previously done by men, including building and painting cars.

The twentieth century has seen huge changes in science and technology, which have affected everyone's lives.

COMPUTERS The first American computer, ENIAC (Electronic Numeric Integrator and Calculator) was so big that it occupied a huge room. Despite its size, it was no more powerful than a small modern home computer.

Today's computers contain *microchips* that allow them to store vast amounts of information. This information can be called up instantly and used to carry out difficult tasks such as making financial calculations, monitoring factory production, drawing up timetables, and designing complex machines. Some computers can even be programmed to control robots which are used in factories to carry out special tasks.

THE COMMUNICATIONS REVOLUTION It is possible for computers to communicate with each other, not simply within one country but even across continents, by using satellites. When two or more computers are linked together this is called a *network*.

More and more office work is being carried out by people who communicate with each other by means of computer terminals and fax machines. In the future, it will be possible for people to see and talk to each via their computer screens.

MEDICINE The Scottish scientist Sir Alexander Fleming discovered penicillin in 1928. It was first available as a medical drug towards the end of World War II. Penicillin is an *antibiotic*. It works by destroying the cell walls of bacteria that cause infection within the human body. Doctors use antibiotics to treat many diseases, like tuberculosis and pneumonia, which were previously responsible for many deaths.

THE BUILDING BLOCKS OF LIFE In 1953, two scientists, James Watson and Francis Crick, identified a mechanism by which all living things pass on genetic characteristics to their offspring. In humans, this substance controls the features, such as hair color or height, that a person inherits from his or her parents. Earlier in the century it had been discovered that the central nucleus of the cells of all living things contain chromosomes that govern the cell's growth and formation.

Watson and Crick discovered that the chemical within the chromosomes, called deoxyribonucleic acid or DNA, was formed of two separate threads coiled around each other in a double helix. In DNA the order of the molecules within the helix forms a chemical code which governs the cell's growth. It is the complex pattern of DNA in cells that indicates differences between the species of plant and animal life, as well as between individuals.

The study of DNA has helped scientists discover more about inherited diseases in humans. By isolating the parts of the DNA that cause such diseases as cystic fibrosis, muscular dystrophy and Down's syndrome, scientists can work towards finding a cure for these and

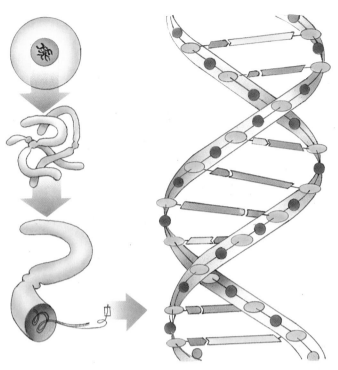

Left. In 1953, James Watson and Francis Crick discovered the structure of the molecule of life – DNA – which is a major part of the chromosomes within our body cells. DNA molecules carry the genetic information which makes our body's cells work. It also carries the genes which give us our particular characteristics, such as whether we have blue or brown eyes, whether we are tall or short, and so on. The structure of DNA is like a spiral ladder. The strands can separate to form new DNA and pass on characteristics. Sometimes this can go wrong, leading to diseases which are inherited by children from their parents.

Above. Information is stored on a compact disc as pits on a plastic dish. A laser reads this and reproduces the sound.

Above. The cassette tape holds information as patterns on a magnetic tape, in this case in a compact cassette.

Invented in 1876 by Alexander Bell, the telephone works on the same principle, although calls are now transmitted as light pulses along optic fibers.

Synthetic rubber is made from chemicals. It can be used to make anything from elastic bands to car tires.

Right. Alexander Fleming discovered the first antibiotic, penicillin, in 1928. He had noticed that some green mold he was growing had prevented bacteria from growing. From this, the antibiotic was developed and has since saved millions of lives. He was awarded the Nobel Prize for Medicine in 1945 along with colleagues Florey and Chain, with whom he worked on specific uses of penicillin.

Organic Transplants

South African surgeon Christiaan Barnard performed the first successful heart transplant operation in 1967. For many years the operation remained risky and many patients died when their bodies rejected the tissue of another human. However, the success rate for heart transplant operations has risen dramatically, with a high percentage of patients surviving and going on to live for 10 or more years after the transplant.

Livers, kidneys, hearts and lungs and bone marrow have now all been transplanted and have helped save many lives.

other diseases. A study of DNA is helping scientists produce crops that are resistant to disease and which have characteristics that enable them to be grown in specific climatic and soil conditions.

One major achievement that has come from research into the structure of cells is the "test tube baby" technique developed by Patrick Steptoe in 1978. An egg was taken from the mother's body and fertilized in a test tube. The growing embryo was later put back inside its mother's womb, where it developed normally. Since it was developed, this technique has helped many childless couples to have children.

Scientists and doctors have made enormous advances in controlling the spread of infectious diseases by a process known as vaccination. In this, an individual's own immune system is primed to counteract a disease by being injected with a tiny quantity of the disease.

In 1955 Dr. Jonas Salk produced a vaccine to prevent polio that has been so successful that the disease, which once crippled many children, is now almost unknown. Other potentially fatal diseases such as typhoid, cholera and smallpox have disappeared from many areas of the world.

But there are always fresh challenges for the medical profession and one of the greatest of these will be how to halt the spread of the AIDS virus – which causes acquired immune deficiency syndrome – and to treat patients who develop the disease.

Much scientific research is concerned with putting people into space, and exploring the outer reaches of the universe. The results can help in everyday life. Teflon for example, was invented for the Apollo space program, and new fabrics came about from space-suit design.

THE RACE TO SPACE

"That's one small step for a man; one giant leap for mankind." These words were spoken by American astronaut Neil Armstrong on July 20, 1969, and told the world that people had landed on the Moon for the first time. Over 500 million viewers around the world watched this event on television.

The successful Apollo 11 mission to the Moon was the result of a race between the Americans and the Russians to see who could become the most technologically advanced nation.

Yuri Gagarin was the first man to travel in space in April 1961.

THE START OF THE RACE A German scientist, Werner von Braun, developed the first high-altitude rocket, called the V2, which was used against Britain towards the end of World War II. After the war, von Braun was invited to the United States to continue his research. However, it was the Russians who made the first breakthrough in space travel on October 4, 1957, when they launched a satellite, *Sputnik I*, into orbit around the Earth. *Sputnik* circled the Earth for 96 days before breaking up.

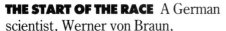

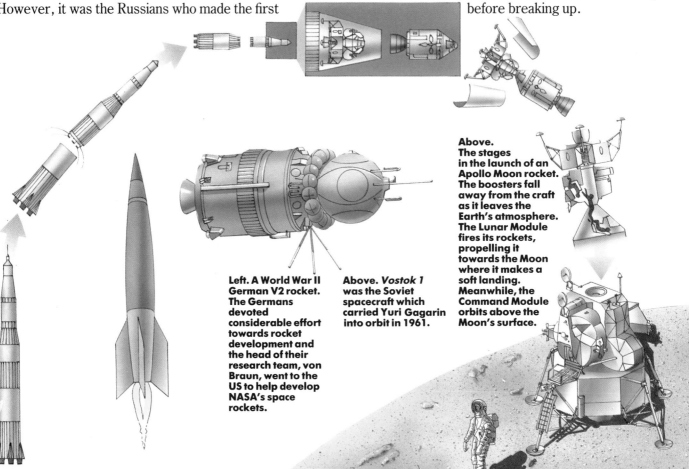

Left. A World War II German V2 rocket. The Germans devoted considerable effort towards rocket development and the head of their research team, von Braun, went to the US to help develop NASA's space rockets.

Above. *Vostok 1* was the Soviet spacecraft which carried Yuri Gagarin into orbit in 1961.

Above. The stages in the launch of an Apollo Moon rocket. The boosters fall away from the craft as it leaves the Earth's atmosphere. The Lunar Module fires its rockets, propelling it towards the Moon where it makes a soft landing. Meanwhile, the Command Module orbits above the Moon's surface.

On April 12, 1961, the Russian cosmonaut Yuri Gagarin became the first person in space. His spacecraft, *Vostok I*, completed one orbit of the Earth. Alan Shepard became the first American to make a space flight three weeks later.

In that same year, President John F. Kennedy set his scientists the challenge of landing people on the Moon by the end of the decade. America put an increasing amount of money into its space program and unmanned spacecraft were sent to photograph and to land on the Moon.

NEW DIRECTIONS After the Moon landings in 1969, Americans sent another five missions there. On these occasions, the astronauts gathered rock samples and even drove a "moon buggy." The last Moon landing was the *Apollo 17* mission in December 1972.

Since then, the US and Soviet space programs have concentrated on building space stations that can stay in orbit around the Earth, and on developing spacecraft that can be used over and over again. Soviet cosmonauts have stayed in space for longer and longer periods, in order to test the effect of weightlessness. In 1988, a Soviet stayed in space for 366 days.

During the 1980s, the United States launched its space shuttle program. This developed a reusable craft, rather like an airplane, to carry passengers and cargo on short flights into space. The shuttle has been used to launch satellites.

THE FUTURE One day, people may colonize the planets in order to mine rare minerals or to create new towns and cities if the Earth becomes too crowded. The technology already exists to build colonies on the Moon or Mars. Food crops could be grown inside clear plastic domes there.

At present, traveling even to the nearest star would take many years.

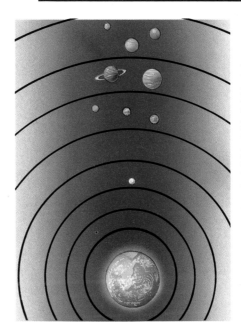

The Solar System

Both the USSR and the USA have launched unmanned craft to explore the planets of our solar system. The *Viking 1* and *2* expeditions have landed on Mars, photographed it and collected soil samples. It is possible that people will land on Mars in the not too distant future.

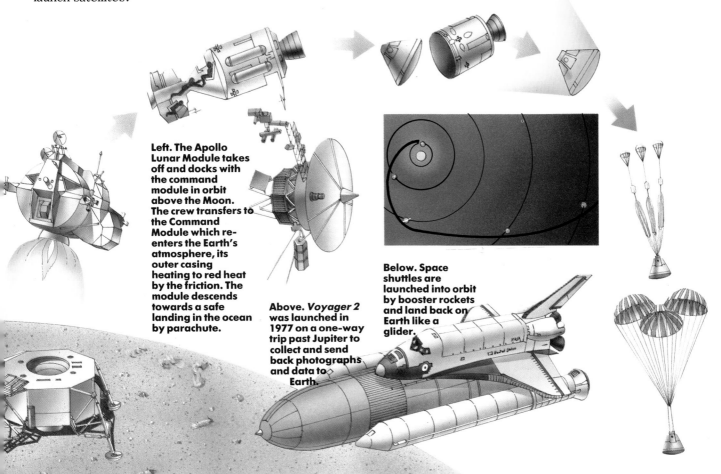

Left. The Apollo Lunar Module takes off and docks with the command module in orbit above the Moon. The crew transfers to the Command Module which re-enters the Earth's atmosphere, its outer casing heating to red heat by the friction. The module descends towards a safe landing in the ocean by parachute.

Above. *Voyager 2* was launched in 1977 on a one-way trip past Jupiter to collect and send back photographs and data to Earth.

Below. Space shuttles are launched into orbit by booster rockets and land back on Earth like a glider.

THE WORLD TODAY

Cutting down the rain forests, such as this one in Guatemala, for farming or development, means fewer trees to absorb the increasing amounts of carbon dioxide being produced.

The greatest problem facing the world today is not war, famine or natural disasters. It is over-population.

POPULATION AND THE ENVIRONMENT In 1991, the world's population was around 5.3 billion. It is expected to rise to around 6.5 billion by the year 2000. In 100 years, the world's population will be more than double its present size. This growth means that people will need to use more natural resources, such as *fossil fuels*, minerals, farming land and timber.

The rate of population increase is highest in developing countries (see page 64). In some of these countries, more than 40 percent of the population is under the age of 16. When they grow up and have children of their own, the results will be far worse poverty, famine and disease than has been seen so far.

THE DEVELOPED WORLD The expanding world population is also threatening developed countries, where more people are living longer and want a better life-style. If this continues, there will be more and more cars on the roads, while factories will be producing more and more goods which use more of the Earth's scarce resources.

Improvements in farming, fishing and industry have helped the developed countries to become wealthy. But people are now realizing that these improvements have disadvantages as well. Farmers use chemical fertilizers which sink into the soil and pollute our water supplies. Modern fishing methods are so effective that not enough fish are surviving to breed, so the numbers of fish are falling. Fish are also being killed by the chemical pollution which factories release into our rivers and seas.

THE GREENHOUSE EFFECT Every year, more and more of the rain forests of South America, Africa and the Far East are being cleared for timber and farming. Some scientists believe that cutting down forests is adding to the amount of carbon dioxide in the Earth's atmosphere, creating a "greenhouse effect" that is raising temperatures worldwide.

These changes in the Earth's climate are causing more land to turn to desert, which means that there are more frequent droughts in countries like Ethiopia and

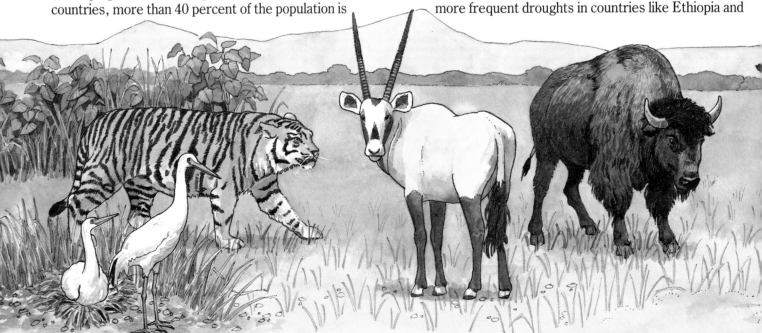

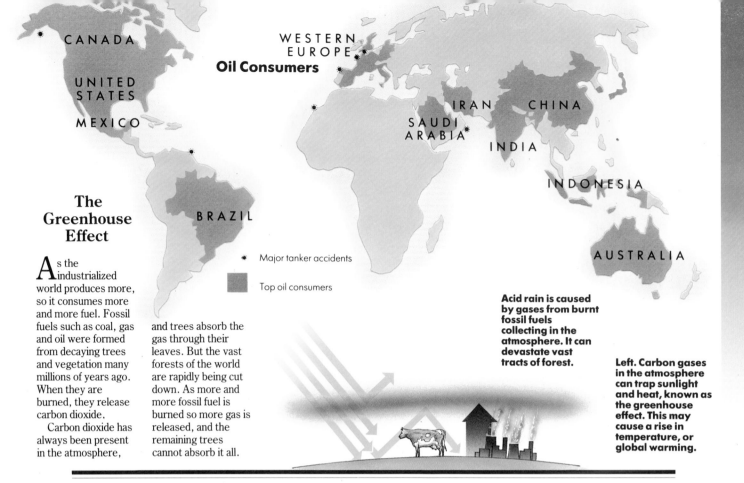

CANADA

WESTERN EUROPE

UNITED STATES

MEXICO

IRAN   CHINA

SAUDI ARABIA

INDIA

INDONESIA

BRAZIL

AUSTRALIA

• Major tanker accidents

Top oil consumers

The Greenhouse Effect

As the industrialized world produces more, so it consumes more and more fuel. Fossil fuels such as coal, gas and oil were formed from decaying trees and vegetation many millions of years ago. When they are burned, they release carbon dioxide.

Carbon dioxide has always been present in the atmosphere, and trees absorb the gas through their leaves. But the vast forests of the world are rapidly being cut down. As more and more fossil fuel is burned so more gas is released, and the remaining trees cannot absorb it all.

Acid rain is caused by gases from burnt fossil fuels collecting in the atmosphere. It can devastate vast tracts of forest.

Left. Carbon gases in the atmosphere can trap sunlight and heat, known as the greenhouse effect. This may cause a rise in temperature, or global warming.

Sudan. Increased temperatures also cause parts of the ice caps at the North and South Poles to melt, which raises the sea level and causes flooding in coastal areas all over the world.

FINDING A SOLUTION The survival of our world will depend not just on stopping the population from growing too fast, but also on greater cooperation between developed and developing countries. At the moment, the Earth's resources are unfairly divided between rich and poor countries, and the demand for consumer goods in western societies threatens to use up all these resources within a few decades. If we can all agree to divide up what we have more equally, and find ways of living which are less wasteful, there is some chance that our planet can recover.

People everywhere will have to use less energy, for example by finding more efficient manufacturing methods, giving up private cars, using public transport and recycling household waste. We will have to make greater use of alternative sources of energy from the Sun, the winds and tides. And of course we will all have to agree to have fewer children, so that we have sufficient resources to care for the children that we do have, in both the rich First World countries and those where food is short.

Humans have been responsible for many species of plants and animals becoming extinct, either through hunting or through the destruction of their natural habitats for farming or development. However, international conservation agencies are doing what they can to save those which are now under severe threat, such as from left the tiger, onyx, bison, white rhino, leather back turtle and Japanese crane.

Creating a New World
TIME CHART

	EUROPE/USA	RUSSIA/CHINA/FAR EAST	MIDDLE EAST	REST OF THE WORLD
AD				
1945	The United Nations is formed with its headquarters in New York			
1946			Formation of the state of Israel	
1948>1949	Berlin is blockaded by the Soviet Union. The Allies have to mount an airlift to supply food to the city			
1949	The formation of the North Atlantic Treat Organization (NATO)	People's Republic of China is proclaimed. Mao Zedong is elected chairman of the people's council (head of state)		
1950>1953		Korean War. USA intervenes to halt the advance of North Korea's Communist forces into South Korea		
1957	The Treaty of Rome: Six European Nations form the Common Market			
1959				Revolution in Cuba – Marxist leader Castro comes to power
1961	The Berlin Wall is built			South Africa becomes a republic
1962				Cuban Missile Crisis
1964			Civil war breaks out in Cyprus	Kenya achieves independence
1967			The Six Day War – Israel is attacked by neighboring Arab states but defeats them	
1965>1973		Vietnam War		
1973			The Yom Kippur War – Arabs launch a surprise attack on Israel which is celebrating the religious feast of Yom Kippur	An extreme right wing coup led by Col. Pinochet sweeps Allende from power in Chile
1979			The Shah of Iran is deposed and Iran becomes an Islamic state	
1979>1989				Soviet invasion and occupation of Afghanistan
1980				The all-white government of Rhodesia concede power to a black majority government and a new constitution. Zimbabwe is born
1982				Falklands conflict
1985		Mikhail Gorbachev becomes leader of the Soviet Union		
1988		China – massacre of anti-communist demonstrators in Tiananmen Square, Bejing		
1989>1990		East Germany's Communist government topples and with it the Berlin Wall. Anti-Communist revolution deposes regimes in Czechoslovakia and Romania		
1991			The Gulf War. Iraq invades Kuwait but is forced out by UN troops in support of a	

72

GLOSSARY

alliance Friendship formed between countries that offer to support each other through trade or military intervention.

antibiotics Drugs that fight bacterial infection.

apartheid South African policy of separating black people from white people. Until recently, laws prevented black people from entering "whites only" areas and made mixed marriages illegal.

armistice Time when opposing armies agree to a permanent cease-fire.

artillery Heavy long-range guns.

balance of power A situation when two or more countries are equal in terms of armed forces and where no side has a military advantage.

Balkan states The Balkans are in the southeast corner of Europe just north of Asia Minor. The states are Greece, Bulgaria, Romania, Albania and the states that are now part of present-day Yugoslavia— Bosnia, Hercegovina, Croatia and Serbia.

bankrupt Having no money and being unable to borrow because creditors have obtained an order to close down your business.

benefits (state) State payments for people who are ill, out of work or who have retired. The money to pay benefits is raised by taxing people who are at work.

blockade When a country sends its army or navy to surround another with the purpose of closing its borders and preventing it trading.

Boer The original Dutch colonists who settled in South Africa.

Bolshevik A member of the Russian Social Democrats who favored revolutionary tactics.

cash crop A single crop that is grown only for the export market. Cash crops are sold to earn money to pay for imported goods. Examples of cash crops include tea, coffee, rubber and sugar.

censorship The suppression of ideas published or broadcast in books, newspapers, films, radio and television that are thought to be immoral or against the interests of the state.

collectivism A political system based upon people coming together in groups to share the benefits of their work.

colony Land that has been taken over and ruled by a foreign country (usually a Western or developed nation).

concentration camp A temporary high-security prison used in wartime to contain people thought to be a danger to the state.

communism A system of government where all power rests in the hands of a single party and which controls all economic activity and provides all social services.

consumer society A society where the freedom of the individual is expressed in his or her power to spend money in whichever way they choose—usually on luxury goods.

coup A sudden strike intended to overthrow a government and spark a revolution.

cubism A school of painting where a subject is seen as a series of interconnected geometric shapes.

democracy A system of government where all political parties supposedly have an equal opportunity to form a government, as in the US.

dictatorship Absolute rule by one leader in a government where there is no opposition, as in Hitler's Germany.

emigrants People who leave one country to settle in another, usually in search of improved economic prospects.

ethnic group People who belong to a recognizable cultural or racial group who have arrived in a country to improve their economic prospects.

exile To force to leave one's native country.

feudal society A society in which the citizens have no property-owning rights and owe a duty to an established aristocracy.

fossil fuels Organic materials that were trapped at a time when prehistoric muds and sands were being compressed to form layers of rock, and which then formed coal, oil or natural gas.

front line The outer limit of territory held secure by an army in battle.

fundamentalist A person who holds strong religious beliefs.

glasnost A Russian word for openness. President Gorbachev used the word to characterize a new spirit of freedom in the Soviet Union.

Hindu A Indian religion.

internal combustion engine An engine which burns fuel such as a car engine.

Islam Religion founded by the prophet Mohammed.

kamikaze Japanese suicide pilot.

mass production A system of manufacturing which breaks the process of construction into stages or small repetitive tasks.

Marxist Someone who believes in Karl Marx's socialist theories.

Menshevik A member of a minority group of the Russian Socialists who opposed the Bolsheviks' violent tactics.

merchant ship A ship that carries cargo.

microchip A small miniaturized component that is part of a computer.

Muslims Followers of the Islamic faith.

napalm A highly inflammable petroleum jelly made into bombs. It was used by the US air force to bomb villages in Vietnam.

network (computer) A series of work stations linked together.

neutral A person or country that is independent and not allied to another.

pension Money paid to people who have retired from work.

perestroika A Soviet word for restructuring, specifically of the Soviet economy.

persecution To subject a person to constant hostility and ill-treatment.

psychoanalysis Method of determining a person's mental state from patterns of behavior which can be subconscious.

recession Extreme decline in economic conditions.

refugee Person who is forced to flee from political persecution.

resistance movement An underground network of freedom fighters operating in a country that is occupied by an enemy power. Resisters often try to sabotage the enemy's war effort by attempting to disrupt industry or transport.

Russian Orthodox A type of Christian religion practiced in Russia.

stock market A place where company shares are bought and sold.

superpower A large nation with considerable world influence, such as the USA and the USSR.

surrealist An artistic movement which portrays images from the unconscious mind in realistic detail.

trade union A workers' organization formed to carry out collective bargaining with employers.

welfare state A country which looks after its people by providing state benefits for those who are ill, retired, sick and so on.

INDEX

Further Reading

GENERAL REFERENCE
The World at War by Mark
Arnold-Forster (Madison,
1986)

*Chronicle of the Twentieth
Century* ed. by Clifton
Daniel (Prentice Hall,
1988)

Atlas of Twentieth Century World History by Michael Dockrill (HarperCollins, 1991)

Twentieth Century: A Brief Global History by Richard Goff (McGraw-Hill, 1990)

The Twentieth Century: A People's History by Howard Zinn (HarperCollins, 1984)

The Twentieth Century by Trevor Cairns (Cambridge, 1984)

A History of Technology: The Twentieth Century ed. by Trevor I. Williams (Oxford, 1978)

Pictorial History of World War I Years by Edward Jablonski (Doubleday, 1985)

Pictorial History of World War II Years by Edward Jablonski (Doubleday, 1985)

EUROPE
Twentieth Century Europe by Alexander Rudhart (Prentice Hall, 1985)

Europe Since 1945: An Introduction by Peter Lane (Barnes & Noble, 1985)

Europe Since 1945: A Concise History by J. Robert Wegs (Saint Martin's, 1990)

Empire to Welfare State: English History 1906–1976 by T. O. Lloyd (Oxford, 1979)

THE UNITED STATES
The Atlas of American History by Robert Ferrell (Facts On File, 1991)

Twentieth Century United States History by Daniel Preston (HarperCollins, 1992)

Twentieth Century America by Irwin Unger (Saint Martin's, 1989)

A Pictorial Story of Our Country by Jerry E. Jennings (Gateway, 1979)

THE REST OF THE WORLD
Arab-Israeli Conflict by Paul Harper (Watts, Franklin, 1990)

The Rise of Modern China by Dorothy Morrison (Longman, 1988)

Picture Acknowledgement

The author and publishers would like to acknowledge, with thanks,
the following photographic sources:

p. 11 (left) Edimedia, (right) Popperfoto; p. 12 Hulton-Deutsch Collection; p. 14 (upper)
Bridgeman Art Library, (lower) Mansell Collection; p. 15 Mary Evans Picture Library; p. 16
Bettmann Archive; p. 17 Ullstein Bilderdienst; p. 19 Camera Press; p. 21 (upper) Hulton-
Deutsch Collection, (lower) Camera Press; p. 22 (upper) ET Archive, (lower) Bettmann Archive;
p. 23 Hulton-Deutsch Collection; p. 24 (upper) Mansell Collection, (lower left) Hulton-Deutsch
Collection, (lower right) SCR Photo Library; p. 25 (upper & lower) SCR Photo Library; p. 26
Mansell Collection, p. 27 (upper) Bettmann Archive, (lower) Mary Evans Picture Library; p. 28
Topham Picture Source; p. 29 (upper) Bridgeman Art Library, (centre) Hulton-Deutsch
Collection, (lower) AKG; p. 30 Hulton-Deutsch Collection, (lower right) AKG; p. 31 (right)
Imperial War Museum, (lower) Illustrated London News Picture Library; p. 33 (upper)
Hulton-Deutsch Collection, (lower) Popperfoto; p. 34 (upper) Imperial War Museum, (centre)
ET Archive; p. 36 Hulton-Deutsch Collection; p. 37 Hulton-Deutsch Collection; p. 38 (upper &
lower) Hulton-Deutsch Collection; p. 39 Camera Press; p. 42 (upper) AKG, (lower) Popperfoto;
p. 43 (upper SCR Photo Library, (lower) Popperfoto; p. 44 (left & centre) Rex Features, (right)
Popperfoto; p. 45 Popperfoto; p. 46 Camera Press; p. 47 (left) Robert Harding Picture Library,
(upper right) Frank Spooner Pictures, (lower right) Rex Features; p. 48 Camera Press; p. 50
Camera Press; p. 51 Topham Picture Source; p. 53 (left, centre & right) Popperfoto; p. 57 (left)
ET Archive, (upper & lower right) Rex Features; p. 58 (upper) SCR Photo Library, (lower) John
Arthur/Impact Photos; p. 61 (upper) Topham Picture Source, (lower left) Orde Eliason/Link,
(right & lower centre) Popperfoto; p. 62 (upper & lower) Kobal Collection; p. 63 (upper)
Bridgeman Art Library, (lower left & right) Camera Press, (lower centre) Hulton-Deutsch
Collection; p. 64 (upper) Mark Edwards/Still Pictures, (centre) Frank Spooner Pictures, (lower)
Hulton-Deutsch Collection; p. 65 Frank Spooner Pictures; p. 66 (upper) IBM, (centre) Ford
Photo Library; p. 67 Hulton-Deutsch Collection; p. 68 Popperfoto; p. 70 Still Pictures. Wherever
possible the copyright holder has been notified but we apologise if any material appears in error.